ZAP

FREE SPEECH AND TOLERANCE IN THE LIGHT OF THE ZERO AGGRESSION PRINCIPLE

Gerard Casey

SOCIETAS
essays in political
& cultural criticism

imprint-academic.com

Published in the UK by
Imprint Academic Ltd., PO Box 200, Exeter EX5 5YX, UK

Distributed in the USA by
Ingram Book Company,
One Ingram Blvd., La Vergne, TN 37086, USA

ISBN 9781788360173 paperback

A CIP catalogue record for this book is available from the
British Library and US Library of Congress

To my son

Gerard Patrick Casey

1985-2017

*Everyone has the right to freedom of opinion and
expression; this right includes freedom to hold opinions
without interference and to seek, receive and impart
information and ideas through any media
and regardless of frontiers*
—*Universal Declaration of Human Rights*

*Tolerance implies no lack of commitment to one's own
beliefs. Rather it condemns the oppression
or persecution of others*
—*John F. Kennedy*

Proclaim the truth and do not be silent through fear.
—*St. Catherine of Siena*

Contents

Foreword and Acknowledgements

Not another book on free speech! Not another book on tolerance! Aren't there plenty of good books on these topics already? Yes indeed, among which I highly recommend Frank Furedi's *On Tolerance*, Nadine Strossen's *Hate* and, on a topic related to the final chapters of this book, Ben Cobley's *The Tribe*. That being so, what, if anything, is the added value of *ZAP*?

I argue that free speech and tolerance are closely related topics and that a defensible treatment of both requires a principled rather than a pragmatic approach. Such an approach, I believe, can be provided by the Zero Aggression Principle (ZAP). This principle permits a defence of free speech to be coherently articulated while simultaneously avoiding the free-for all that would result from adopting a fundamentalist approach to free speech, as well as firmly rejecting the current *ad hoc* measures that are operative in our societies. The ZAP also provides the basis for a coherent and defensible account of tolerance.

I also argue that the currently fashionable dogmas of diversity, inclusion and equality are pre-eminent practical manifestations of intolerance and are therefore properly to be exposed and criticised as such.

Although the elements of a critical account such as this have been around for some time, I don't believe that anyone has grounded an approach to free speech and tolerance on the same basic principle while also characterising and criticising the fashionable doctrines of diversity, inclusion and equality as instances of practical intolerance. If they have, I'm not aware of it but I apologise if I've inadvertently repeated what has been done elsewhere. I console myself with the thought that if it's worth doing, it's worth doing twice!

I'm not sure if many people will like this book. I'm not sure if I like it myself but, as Ralph Vaughan Williams is reputed to have said about one of his symphonies, 'I don't know whether I like it, but it's what I meant.' I suspect that my libertarian friends (some of them, at least) will baulk at my imperfectly concealed socially conservative views while my conservative friends (all of them) will object to my overtly libertarian approach. Free speech fundamentalists will be appalled at my suggestion that there are *any* limits to free speech and my Christian co-believers may wonder (if they haven't already) if I've abandoned my faith and become a sceptic, a relativist and a libertine. To libertarians and conservatives I would reply that libertarianism and conservatism are compatible, to free speech fundamentalists I would point out that liberty is not licence, and to my fellow Christians I can only say that I believe more firmly than ever I did in the way, the life and the truth.

I have tried to keep this book focussed on practical issues and not allow it to float away on a sea of philosophical abstractions. As will be evident from even a cursory reading of this book, I have ransacked newspapers and other print and online sources for material germane to my project. A perennial danger in trying to be topical is that there's always another story, always another incident that just has to be included so that no matter where one stops the discussion one is sure to be overtaken by events. The manuscript as published was completed in May 2019. In striving to keep the discussion grounded (popular) while providing some measure of analysis (criticism), my plan was to provide two stools for the reader to sit on but I cannot shake off a nagging suspicion that the reader may end up trying to sit on the empty space between them.

The writing project, of which this book is a part, was originally conceived as a joint venture with my friend and colleague Tim Crowley but my would-be partner in crime was unable to continue. We have, however, been in regular correspondence and some of his ideas and, I suspect, even some of his *ipsissima verba* may have found their way into the finished work. Thanks for the inspiration and support, Tim, and apologies for any inadvertent plagiarism.

The References section contains a list of books, articles and online material that I consulted in the writing of this book. I don't agree with everything in all of these writings—that would be little short of miraculous!—but I have found what their authors had to say informative, consciousness-raising, enlightening, sometimes infuriating but always stimulating.

I believe that all the statements made in this book about named or identifiable individuals are substantially true. In almost every such case, these statements are a re-publication, either verbatim or in paraphrase, of reports already available in the public domain. In any event, statements made in this book are my honest opinions and are made in the public interest.

I thank those who unselfishly gave of their time to read over my manuscript, in particular Patricia Casey and Mary Newman. Apart from readers' substantive suggestions for improvement—the one about using the manuscript to fuel the incinerator was perhaps a little harsh!—they have pointed out typographical errors, stylistic infelicities and instances of more than usual incomprehensibility. If any of these remain, it's entirely their fault!

And a special word of thanks is due to Jason Walsh for help well above and beyond the call of either duty or friendship.

How Free Should Free Speech Be?

I believe there are more instances of the abridgment of the freedom
of the people by gradual and silent encroachments of those in
power than by violent and sudden usurpations.
—James Madison

Don't teach tricks to your girlfriend's dog or, at least, don't teach him certain kinds of tricks. A Scottish YouTube comedian, Mark Meechan (aka Count Dankula) shot his girlfriend's dog raising his (the dog's) paw while Meechan made pro-Nazi comments. The shooting was done with a camera, I hasten to add, not with a gun! The video, pretty obviously a joke even if the joke was in bad taste, was posted online and was visited over three million times. Not everyone was amused, however. Meechan was taken to court and convicted in 2018 under the Communications Act of grossly offensive behaviour by inciting racial hatred! There had been no complaints from the public so it seems that the only ones not to get the joke were the police officers and the court officials.

Meechan explained during his trial that he wasn't a Nazi but did he really have to? Would any self-respecting card-carrying Nazi teach a *dog* to give the Nazi salute? Meechan claimed that he posted the video to annoy his girlfriend. Well, that's very bad boyfriend behaviour indeed—tut, tut, Mr Meechan—but it hardly makes his action anti-Semitic and racist, which is what the court sheriff declared it to be. The only ray of light in this whole affair was that at least the RSPCA didn't prosecute Meechan for animal abuse but maybe they're just biding their time!

A little light Libertarianism

Should you be able to say anything you like, to anyone, at any time, anywhere, in public or in private, in person or electronically, even if you have to get your girlfriend's dog to do it for you? How would *you* answer this question? With a 'Yes', with a 'No', or with an 'It depends'? Think about your answer for a minute or two before reading on. No, seriously, really do think about it for a minute or two.

In the contemporary world, the problems associated with adjudicating free speech issues can seem intractable, a matter of clashing and mutually inconsistent rights. But almost all the problems associated with free speech and the restrictions to which it may be subjected (if any) stem from our not having a principled basis on which to make coherent and consistent decisions. Some principle or other has to be found to determine what we may say and where and how we may say it if, on the one hand, our speech is not to be subject to the capricious whims of those in authority or the soft tyranny of the Twitterati or if, on the other hand, we are not to fall under the sway of free speech fundamentalists (of which I'm not one) who recognise no limitations of any kind on speech in any circumstances.

This book is written from a libertarian perspective. Like that renowned political philosopher, Michael Corleone, 'I have no intention of placing my fate in the hands of men whose only qualification is that they managed to con a block of people to vote for them'. (Puzo, 366) However, I also have to live in the world as it actually is (as we all must do) so the discussion and analysis that follows will occasionally take into account where we actually are on the matter of free speech as distinct from where we might (if we were libertarians) wish to be. Given the centrality of libertarianism to the following discussion and analysis, it might be a good idea to give readers unacquainted with it a brief account of its essentials.

Libertarianism is the philosophical and political position that takes as its grounding the fundamental importance of freedom in inter-human relations—the clue is in the name! From the libertarian perspective, individual freedom forms the necessary and ineliminable context of all mature and responsible social relations. The primary social implication of libertarianism may be expressed, positively and informally, in the claim that you have the right, subject to certain minimal conditions, to do whatever you wish provided only that, in so doing, you do not infringe on the like right of others. Negatively, and more precisely, the basic operative principle that governs human interactions without the requirement for consent is the Zero Aggression Principle (ZAP): *No one may initiate or threaten to initiate aggression* [coercive physical violence] *against the person or property of another.*

It should be noted that what is ruled out by the ZAP is the *initiation* of aggression (such as murder, rape, theft, assault) or the threat to initiate such aggression against the person or property of another; libertarianism does *not* rule out the use of violence in *defence* of one's person or property *against* aggression. The practical difficulties of telling the difference in borderline cases between aggression (which libertarianism prohibits) and the forceful resistance of aggression (which libertarianism permits) doesn't tell against the clear conceptual difference between the two. As part of your fundamental freedom, you have the right to defend your most basic property, yourself, and any other property that you have rightfully acquired. Of course, you may waive that right if you wish so that pacifism and libertarianism are compatible although libertarianism doesn't require pacifism.

There is something startlingly obvious about the ZAP. We learn as children not to hit other children and not to take what belongs to them, not least because *we* object to being hit ourselves and to having *our* stuff taken! All parents know that not long after their little darlings learn to speak and start to play with other children, they can expect to hear 'He took my toys' and 'She started it' and 'That's not fair'. This is kids' stuff and libertarianism is, in a sense, simply kids' stuff writ large. A critic once remarked that Libertarianism is the philosophy of 3-year olds! That remark was meant to be dismissive but I take it to be a back-handed insight into the obviousness of the ZAP, the truth of which is so patent that even 3-year old children can understand it.

Obvious the ZAP may be but, when examined, it turns out to rest on a certain conception of property—specifically, it rests on the, perhaps initially startling, claim that we own ourselves and, as the rightful owners of ourselves, only we can rightfully decide what is to be done by and to our bodies and our minds. If you hit Tom, it is aggression against Tom because Tom has a property right in his person. The concept of self-ownership may seem to be a characteristically modern idea but in fact it was clearly articulated as long ago as the high Middle Ages. The medieval master of the University of Paris, Henry of Ghent, in a 1289 discussion of whether a man condemned to death could lawfully flee, argued that whereas others might have the right to use the criminal's body in certain ways, only the criminal himself had a property right in his own body. Henry used the word *proprietas* to describe this right, not the more common (and ambiguous) word *dominium*. The criminal's efforts of self-preservation (provided he did not thereby injure another) were equitable (*fas*), permitted by the law of nature and therefore licit (*licitum*) and right (*ius*) and, Henry argues, even a matter of necessity (*necessitas*).

We don't perhaps normally think of ourselves as something that can be owned but the libertarian self-ownership claim is, minimally, a rejection of the idea that anyone else owns us. (In the context of this book, I am concerned only with the this-worldly aspects of ownership and I prescind entirely from theological questions of whether and to what extent a creator God might be said to own his creation and his creatures.) The corollary of owning yourself is that as a free adult person you are also responsible for yourself. Apart from specific agreements, no one else is, or can be, legally obliged to protect, defend, pay for, support, feed, clothe, or care for you. Besides owning yourself, you can own and use anything that you rightfully appropriate that belongs to no one else or anything that you can persuade someone else to transfer to you either by sale or gift. It follows from this that if you liberate Angela's apple from her possession without her consent and convert it to your own purposes, this is trespass, a form of aggression, because Angela owns the apple and it is just as much an act of aggression as if you pulled Angela's hair.

Libertarianism may be justified by an appeal to consequences. One might, for example, claim that the preservation and expansion of the sphere of human liberty will lead to greater prosperity and efficiency. Also, libertarianism might be justified by an appeal to natural law or natural rights. One might, for example, claim that the preservation and expansion of the sphere of human liberty is justified by the nature of man and the nature of the world in which he lives, irrespective of consequences. Although the differences between the two approaches may be reconcilable and even though I am persuaded that the preservation and expansion of the sphere of human liberty would in fact be more beneficial than otherwise, nevertheless, the approach I take to libertarianism is rights-based rather than consequences-based.

Finally, it is important to realise that libertarianism is not, nor is it intended to be, a complete moral theory. Much confusion will be prevented and many possible objections can be summarily deflected if this point is appreciated. Many activities that are currently banned or prohibited by the State—the ingestion of exotic chemical substances, various imaginative forms of consensual sexual congress, non-coerced contractual relations between consenting adults such as prostitution—would all be *legally* permissible from a libertarian perspective, provided, of course, that no violation of the ZAP was involved. The libertarian *as libertarian* makes no judgement on the morality of such acts. That such activities should not be legally prohibited doesn't mean that they are necessarily morally defensible or good or edifying or even sensible. Libertarians can (and do) make moral judgements on many such matters but unless the subject matter of those judgements impinges on human freedom, they do so not wearing their libertarian hats but some other form of moral headgear.

'My house, my rules'

The libertarian maxim for speech that can be derived from the ZAP is 'My House, My Rules' (MHMR), a maxim that is at once both permissive and restrictive. The regulation of speech (and conduct generally) is primarily a matter for the owners of property. On my property or with my property, I can, with certain minimal exceptions, say (and do) what I please (permissive); you may exclusively determine what can be said (and done) on *your* property (permissive). On the other hand, if I were to invite someone to a dinner party at my house and he wanted to make vile racist remarks, I should ask him to cease and desist. If he protested 'But I have a right to free speech' I should say, 'Yes, of course. Now go and speak freely elsewhere!' (restrictive) The same restrictions can be enforced by you on your property. It follows from the maxim MHMR that no one may prevent you by

force or the threat of force from speaking freely on property that is
yours or prevent you from granting permission to others to use your
property as you determine, nor may they prevent you from speaking
freely on any property whose owner has given you the requisite
permission. It also follows from the maxim MHMR that you may
not be compelled to grant a licence to anyone to use your property as
they may wish for purposes of speech or action.

What if you are not minded to accept the ZAP (and its derivative maxim MHMR) as constituting the appropriate parameter for
freedom in general and for freedom of speech in particular? If you
reject the ZAP then you must be prepared in principle to accept the
legitimacy of using physical violence against the person or property
of another or to have others do so on your behalf in circumstances
other than that of resisting aggression. Perhaps more significantly,
you must also be prepared to accept the legitimacy of having others
use physical violence *against you* or *your property* when *you* are not
engaged in aggression! It is possible to reject the ZAP without
lapsing into intellectual incoherence but to do so in practice is to
play a zero-sum power game of winner-takes-all. Lose this game and
the winners may treat you as they wish and you will have no principled grounds for complaint. I think it is true to say that the laws that
currently govern our right to speak freely in most Western democra-
cies are largely a hodgepodge of *ad hoc* measures erected upon no
coherent principled foundation. If you reject the ZAP, you must
either accept this legal goulash or propose some other *principled* basis
upon which freedom and freedom of speech might be erected. And
what would that look like?

The matter of free speech becomes complicated in our current
non-libertarian societies when we come to consider what may or
may not be said in so-called public spaces. Even here, however, the
effective owner of such spaces, which is the person who has the power
to make decisions, is the one who has the right to decide who may
use that property for all purposes, including that of speech. Public
spaces are in effect owned by those who control them, usually
local authorities or national bodies. Where, as would be the case
in a libertarian society, streets, schools, and parks are owned by

individuals or by communities, those individuals or communities will make the rules. It should be emphasised that while the effective owners of such spaces have the right to make such decisions, it doesn't necessarily follow that the decisions that they make will be right! What of institutions in receipt of government money, such as most universities? If there are conditions attached to the receipt of government funding, then the receiver of such funding is contractually bound by those conditions. Otherwise, and outside specific freely assumed conditions, the owners of such institutions have the right, as does any other owner of property, to make decisions on the basis of MHMR.

It follows from the MHMR maxim that having a right to speak freely doesn't carry with it the right to make use of other people's property or resources to enable you to express your views. If others refuse to grant you permission to use their resources this, while it may be foolish or regrettable or petty or mean-spirited, is not, strictly speaking, censorship. On this point, I'm likely to part company with many free speech advocates. In the *Washington Post*, Christine Emba takes issue with writers who claim that editorial control over their columns amounts to a form of censorship. One such writer is Daniella Greenbaum who used to have a column on the website *Business Insider*. Greenbaum resigned from her position because she believed herself to be a victim of censorship when a column she wrote was removed from *Business Insider*'s site for not meeting editorial standards and because it was suggested that what were deemed to be 'culturally sensitive columns' should be reviewed by a second editor. Emba writes, 'But Greenbaum is wrong. The removal of her piece does not mean that writers everywhere are being fallen upon by a "predatory mob," that they are now constantly subject to "intimidation," or even that her "commonsensical opinions" are now "beyond the pale of acceptable opinion." It does not mean, as she seems to imply, there is a looming crisis of free speech. All it means is that Business Insider did not want Daniella Greenbaum's column.' (Emba 2018)

Emba is right, at least in this respect, that one's right to speak freely does not entitle one to a platform on which to speak. The property of others is their property and they and only they may determine who gets to use it for any given purpose, including that of writing and publishing newspaper columns. Another's refusal to publish your material isn't necessarily a curtailment of your right to speak freely. Emba again: '"Free speech," she says, 'does not mean "the right to say whatever you want without criticism on social media," or even "the right to run your columns without being subject to executive decision-making." It means "freedom to speak." Which Greenbaum clearly has, whether she's published by Business Insider or not.' (Emba 2018) Similarly, one's right to free speech doesn't entail that others may not criticise one—in fact, in having a right to free speech, they have exactly that right.

There are those who believe that free speech is under threat from do-gooders who want to prevent anybody being offended anywhere, anytime or by anyone; from politicians who want to appease vocal minorities (religious or ethnic); from university authorities (and students) who believe that students have a right not to have their fragile minds disturbed; from social justice warriors of every stripe; from gender feminists; from transgender activists—in short, from all those who wish to limit the freedom of others to speak freely because *they* know what is good for everyone else and are determined to enforce their views and to prevent the expression of opposing views.

Not everybody is persuaded that free speech is under some kind of dire existential threat. Sam Leith expresses his scepticism on the matter. In his lambent if vulgar phrase, the concern over the alleged devastation being wrought on our freedom of speech is 'essentially, horseshit'. For Leith, free speech is already abridged substantially, *de facto* by good manners and social consensus and *de jure* by defamation laws, laws prohibiting incitement to violence and by the regulation of false advertising. He recognises that the law now limits speech by means of laws on hate speech, Holocaust denial and modern forms of blasphemy but, he says, 'We can and should argue about the limits law places on public discourse—I favour the barest minimum—but we should recognise that is what we are doing, rather than invoking an imaginary, unproblematic ideal called "free speech".' (Leith 2018)

I find myself agreeing in part with Leith though perhaps not for his reasons. I recognise, as he does, and commend in principle the informal social regulation of speech which, in effect, amounts to permitting one to say whatever one likes provided one is prepared to take the social consequences, which might be banishment from polite society and, if especially egregious, ostracism. 'If you say something offensive,' Leith writes, 'you may well suffer an influx of angry eggs; turn up at a costume party blacked up or dressed as a Wehrmacht officer and unless your host is Taki you can expect to cop some flak. But you won't go to jail.' Just so. This is the kind of informal social control that excited J. S. Mill's concerns in *On Liberty*, far more than any overt legal restrictions that might have been imposed by government. Mill was concerned that the extent of such informal social control might become so extensive as to restrict not just overt vulgarity or uncalled-for abrasive or insulting comments but to induce a kind of radical self-censorship. That self-censorship would mean that even polite and warranted, albeit unwelcome, comments on issues of political and social concern would become functionally inexpressible. This is still, I believe, an issue that, with some justification, troubles many of those who are now concerned with the issue of the restriction or limitation of free speech. I recognise, as Leith does, but without necessarily endorsing them, the legal sanctions that already apply to speech, including defamation, incitement to violence and the like. I am not sanguine about the introduction of laws prohibiting 'hate speech' nor am I enthusiastic about the re-introduction of laws prohibiting what is in effect the modern equivalent of blasphemy. I shall discuss these matters in more detail below.

Limitations on free speech?

So, back to my initial question. Are there, or should there be, any limits at all to free speech other than MRMH? Yes, where speech shades over into action and that action is clearly criminal when evaluated by the standard of the ZAP.

The common law distinguishes three inchoate crimes—incitement, conspiracy and attempt. *Attempt* is clearly criminal; the ZAP prohibits not just aggression but the initiation of aggression which is what attempt clearly is. *Conspiracy* may be criminal if it is correctly judged to be the beginnings of a concerted action. On the other hand, it might be nothing more than reprehensible idle talk. *Incitement*, however, is not criminal at all, unless my suggestions somehow have the magical quality of overbearing the autonomy of other human agents and forcing them to do things they wouldn't otherwise do. Incitement is a 'go on' activity rather than a 'come on'. If I post a piece on Facebook saying, 'I think it would be a good idea to burn down the Houses of Parliament' and others go ahead and burn them down, I'm not responsible for what they've done. I'm not a Svengali with the power to overrule other people's wills. The Henry II/Thomas Beckett case lies on the margins between the mere expression of a wish and a command for the king's wish is often taken to be a command. Was Henry, as he said those immortal words, 'Who will rid me of this troublesome priest?' expressing a disinterested question about future possibilities or was he giving a 'wink, wink, nudge, nudge,' implicit command? On the other hand, if my Facebook post reads: 'OK gang, let's go and burn down the Houses of Parliament. Meet outside the entrance to Westminster Abbey at 3.00 p.m. next Saturday. Bring torches and a plentiful supply of petrol. Bottles to make Molotov Cocktails will be provided,' this begins to look like a conspiracy shading over into the beginnings of attempt. There is no mechanical way to determine when such speech passes over into criminal action. The presumption should be that speech is not criminal unless the circumstances, as evaluated by the judgement of normal people, determine otherwise. To recapitulate, by the standards of the ZAP, attempt is clearly criminal and conspiracy may or may not be, depending on circumstances, whereas incitement isn't criminal at all.

What of the civil laws that restrict free speech? What of laws against defamation, for example? English law on defamation (libel or slander) is tortious by definition and tortuous in practice. In general, the law permits (or has permitted) civil actions to be taken in respect of published statements that are alleged to cause a person who is named, or who is otherwise identifiable, to suffer loss in his employment or to lower the reputation of that person in the opinion of right-thinking people. The presumption in law is (or has been) that defamatory statements are false, placing the onus on the defendant to prove them true. Defendants in defamation cases have been able to plead that the published statements were in fact true or that they could have been held to be true by a reasonable person. Statements made in Parliament or in the courts are privileged and are not normally actionable, nor are statements that can be shown to have been made in the public interest. The law was reformed by the Defamation Act 2013 (see National Archives) and now provides for the defences of truth, honest opinion and public interest. Additional, albeit complicated, defences are available for privilege (absolute or qualified) and for material published in scholarly publications and there is a head-wreckingly complicated defence available to website operators. Despite these welcome changes, the law on defamation in England (and to a lesser extent elsewhere in the world) still constitutes an impediment to free speech.

In a libertarian society, there would be no place for defamation laws. Your reputation is what other people think of you and what other people think of you is ultimately a matter for them. You cannot force or require people to think of you in a certain way, however much you might wish them to do so. It might be objected, people's reputations can suffer as the result of defamatory statements and sometimes even their livelihoods can also be deleteriously affected so shouldn't the law prevent or punish such statements? The libertarian answer, in brief, is no.

Truth should be an absolute defence to any proceedings for defamation and any test of lowering the standing of X in the eyes of right-thinking people or its equivalent has to go. If what is said about you is embarrassing or reputation-damaging but true, so be it. Morally, a strong case can be made against detraction (the propagation of true but reputation-damaging statements) but libertarianism draws a sharp distinction between morals and law. Many actions are judged to be immoral but only a subset of them are or should be illegal. Someone might concede the point about truth as a defence but might contend that if what is said about you is false and known to be so by the teller, it would be appropriate to have laws that could punish such egregious untruth-tellers. Again, the libertarian demurs.

To make the essential point once again, your reputation is what other people think of you and you have no right to have them think any particular thing about you.

Is there then no defence against the reputational damage that may be caused by liars or tellers of untruths? Yes. First of all, in a libertarian society in which there were no defamation laws, the presumption that what is published is true (since, were it otherwise, the publishers would run the risk of legal action) would cease to hold. Without defamation laws we would witness a change of culture. There would be no presumption of truth in respect of any claims published in any source and one would be thrown back on accepting the responsibility for determining what to believe for oneself. Secondly, there is nothing to prevent a libertarian society (or any other society for that matter) from operating one or more privately-run fact-checking validation agencies that would do what civil courts do in vindicating your reputation but without their absurd costs and their interminable delays. These agencies would be unimpeachably disinterested bodies and their findings would be eagerly consulted by those with an interest in one's standing and they would do for one's reputation what consumer magazines do for products. Failure by persons making allegations against you to attend the hearings of such agencies or failure to prove, against the presumption of their falsity, the truth of their claims would result in a declaration of the falsity of those claims which would be widely published by such agencies. Third, as things stand, defamation law has a chilling effect on reputable sources but little or no effect on disreputable sources, for example, the lunatic fringe on the internet. (Does it have any other fringe? Think of the comment pages on the internet—who takes them seriously?) In a fully libertarian society, then, there would be no laws of defamation. In current or transitional societies, defamation laws will continue to operate but they should be made as liberal and as limited as possible and availed of only in the most extreme of circumstances.

But surely we have the right not to be gratuitously offended, don't we? No, we don't! There is no such right. Who, after all, is to determine objectively what is and what isn't offensive? In a cohesive society, social conventions, manners and etiquette will generally do a good job in setting limits to the extent of offensive speech. In a society slowly disintegrating, law is dragged into the fray and the giving and taking of offence becomes a toy of fickle legislators. It might be argued that people shouldn't make offensive comments and so it doesn't much matter if we have laws outlawing such comments! Once again, the libertarian distinction between law and morality comes into play. The *shouldn't* in 'people shouldn't make offensive comments' is **moral** but the outlawing *is* **legal**. I shouldn't swear or commit adultery or drink to excess either but do we really want to make swearing or adultery or excessive drinking or whatever our current normative environment considers morally reprehensible to be punishable by law? Some people in some countries that are located in a galaxy not all that far, far away do in fact do this or want to do this but societies based on Western principles have to date been able to resist, at least partially, that siren call. In rejecting the idea that we have a right not to be offended, I do not deny that words can hurt. Who likes to be called by rude names? But however hurtful words may be, there is still a difference in kind, not just in degree, between hurtful words and a hurtful punch in the face.

What of free speech that isn't merely offensive but which is downright hateful? Shouldn't *that* be prohibited? No! Legal prohibition is not in order here either. So I may speak hatefully? Yes, on your own property or on the property of others with their permission and under licence. But a complete answer to this question requires its own treatment. (cf. chapter 2)

Ways of restricting speech

Now that we've got those preliminary issues sketched out, let's turn our attention to some examples of the specific ways in which free speech may be restricted. Free speech tends to come under attack from three angles: first, from informal and unofficial restrictions; second, from self-imposed restrictions (entirely understandable and even perhaps excusable if regrettable in today's censorious culture where saying or even thinking the wrong thing can lose you your job and perhaps even land you in court) and, third, from official state-sponsored, state-enforced censorship, the only kind of restriction that can properly be called censorship, though we might regard the other two kinds of restriction on free speech as forms of semi-censorship.

Almost every society that has ever existed has engaged in some form of censorship. What is censored has, of course, varied over time; so much so that yesterday's heterodoxy tends to become today's orthodoxy and yesterday's orthodoxy today's heterodoxy. Of these three ways of restricting speech, the informal kind, the kind J. S. Mill feared, is probably the most pervasive and the most potent. But official censorship hasn't gone away, you know. We'll see many examples of this during the course of the book but here are a few just to whet your appetite.

In 2016, the Provincial Prosecutor of Valencia initiated criminal proceedings against the Archbishop of Valencia, charging him with inciting 'hate crimes'. The Archbishop had said in a sermon, that 'We have legislation contrary to the family, the action of political and social forces, with added movements and actions of the gay empire, of ideas such as radical feminism, or the most insidious of all, gender theory'. The LGBT collective which filed the complaint said that the Cardinal's words are 'full of hatred, homophobic and sexist, and only incite hatred against those who do not fit into the archaic models defended by the Catholic hierarchy.'

In June of 2005, Pastor Ake Green of Borgholm Pentecostal Church in Sweden was sentenced to a month in prison for preaching against homosexuality. Green did not advocate aggression towards homosexuals but simply restated the biblical understanding of homosexual activity as intrinsically evil. This was considered sufficient to warrant a guilty verdict and time in gaol during which the errant pastor could reflect on his evil ways.

In May 2019, Singapore passed a law (Prevention from Online Falsehoods and Manipulation Bill) directed against the propagation of 'fake news'. Online platforms will have to carry corrections or remove content that the Singaporean government considers to be false. Persons convicted under the Bill (now Act) face prison terms of up to 10 years or fines of up to one million Singaporean dollars. The Director of the International Commission of Jurists. Frederick

Rawski, said that 'The severe penalties proposed under the bill, its broad scope of territorial jurisdiction and the absence of clear protections for expression pose real risks that it will be misused to clamp down on the free exchange and expression of opinions and information.'

In the early 2000s, the Reverend Stephen Boissoin wrote to his local newspaper in Canada objecting to what he called 'the homosexual agenda'. In 2008, he was convicted by a one-person panel of the Alberta Human Rights Tribunal who fined him $5,000 and ordered him never to say anything disparaging about homosexuality again, whether on radio, TV, in church, by email or in letters to the newspapers. The fact that Alberta's human-rights law declares that 'nothing ... shall be deemed to interfere with the free expression of opinion on any subject' cut no ice with the one-man panel. In a move that can only delight aficionados of *Catch-22*-style manoeuvres, the panellist rejected Boissoin's free-speech defence by opining that 'there appeared to be no raging debate in the community at the time the letter was published.' How could there be a debate if one side in any possible debate is censored on the grounds that there's no debate? After a series of hearings, the Alberta Court of Appeal eventually exonerated Mr Boissoin, some ten years after the start of the matter! 'Matters of morality,' Mr Justice Clinton O'Brien said for the Court, 'including the perceived morality of certain types of sexual behavior, are topics for discussion in the public forum ... Freedom of speech does not just protect polite speech'. To which we can only say, 'Amen'.

And then we have the other forms of restriction which may look like censorship but which, strictly speaking, aren't or are, at best, a kind of semi-censorship. You might remember that, on the MHMR maxim, people have a right to do with their property what they wish and that includes declining to use it in certain ways or refusing to allow others to use it. In early 2018, Vue, a large cinema chain in the UK, declined to screen a film entitled 'Voices of the Silenced'. The subject of the film is the extent to which all of us, including Christians, have come under pressure to adapt to what one of my colleagues once called 'the new, normative environment,' in particular, pressure not just to tolerate but to actively approve of the liberal agenda in respect of homosexuality and transsexualism. The cinema chain's action came in response to complaints from Stonewall, the gay rights charity, which claimed that the film promoted gay-cure therapy. It's not unreasonable to take it that Vue's action was prompted by the currently fashionable demonisation of traditional sexual morality, either on their own part or perhaps responding to pressure from groups like Stonewall that share that hostile attitude to traditional sexual morality. Criticisms of the contemporary normalisation of what had not so long ago been widely viewed as abnormal or deviant modes of sexuality are now treated not just as if they were wrong but as if they were positively evil. Some critics characterised Vue's action as a form of censorship but Vue deny the charge, arguing that they are a private organisation and are acting within their rights in declining to offer services to groups with whose views they disagree. I believe Vue are right about being within their rights. In the light of the MHMR maxim, I fully support the right of any person or group to decide the terms on which others may make use of their property. From that point of view, Vue were entirely within their rights to decline to show this film. Of course, whether it was right for Vue to do what it did is quite another matter.

Virgin Trains made a decision in 2017 to stop selling the *Daily Mail*. Some saw this as an act of censorship; others argued that the company had a perfect right to sell or not sell whatever papers it chose. I am sympathetic to those who regard Virgin's actions as a form of censorship but I think they fail to grasp the essential point that people, individually or in companies, have the right to do with their property as they wish. Virgin's decision wasn't just a bland commercial decision but would appear to have been motivated by a distaste for what the *Mail* stands for. In January 2018, the boss of Virgin Trains, Sir Richard Branson, instructed the firm to restock the paper pending a review. In a blogpost, he said, 'Freedom of speech, freedom of choice and tolerance for differing views are the core principles of any free and open society ... While Virgin Trains has always said that their passengers are free to read whatever newspaper they choose on board West Coast trains, it is clear that on this occasion the decision to no longer sell the Mail has not been seen to live up to these principles.'

Two kinds of people

People can be divided into two kinds: those who divide people into two kinds and those who don't! Joking aside, when it comes to free speech, people really can be divided into two kinds. One kind lives by the VOLTAIRE principle—I disapprove of and am offended by what you say, but I will defend to the death your right to say it. (I know that Voltaire didn't say this but the sentiment is customarily attributed to him.) The other kind lives by the ERIATLOV principle—I disapprove of and am offended by what you say and I will defend to the death (of free speech) my right to stop you saying it.

It is interesting to note just how little confidence the Eriatlov's of this world have in the power of reason to arbitrate the truth claims of disputed positions. You would think that a robust Eriatlover would say something like, 'Bring on your stupid and ridiculous beliefs and let me show you in a dazzling display of intellectual pyrotechnics just how stupid and ridiculous they are.' But alas, we usually wait in vain for such a challenge. It is hardly surprising to find the lack of confidence placed in reason by the Eriatlovers of this world because for them, feelings, their feelings at least, are what take centre stage. All else must bow before how they feel and nothing must be allowed to disturb the even tenor of their ways. If a free-thinker lives by the motto, 'Think for yourself', an Eriatlover lives by the motto, 'Think of yourself'.

It used to be that radicals were at the forefront in the demand for free speech. Not any more. Now, one's radicalness is displayed by demanding that anything that might hurt your feelings or offend your sensibilities or the feelings and sensibilities of those whom you have constituted yourself a defender or is hateful (according to you) must be prevented from being expressed. And what precisely is hurtful, offensive or hateful? Ah well, as they used to say in childhood, 'that's for me (the Eriatlover) to know and you to find out'! And it's at this point that self-censorship usually comes in. When you don't know what statements, claims and comments might be taken to invite informal or formal censure and sanction, the only thing to do is to keep quiet. As the old Irish maxim has it, 'Whatever you say, say nothing!'

Those glorious days when to be young was very heaven and to be on the left side of the political spectrum was to challenge censorship and intolerance have vanished like the snows of yesteryear. To be on the left now is to endorse censorship and to censure. Now that the traditional targets of leftist ire have largely disappeared from view, what is there for sinistrals to get excited about? Ah, but you see, there are new outrages that must be challenged or, in the argot of today, 'called out,' in particular, racism (which is seemingly ubiquitous and ineradicable), sexism (equally ubiquitous and ineradicable), homophobia, transphobia and whatever other forms of phobia that are yet to be revealed. The sanctimoniousness of the new censors is every bit as nauseating as was that of the old. Those who sin against the new orthodoxies are not just wrong or misguided but evil! The defenders of the new orthodoxy, having right on their side and being full of good intentions, cannot vilify their opponents with enough vigour. By way of light relief, let's look at another example of semi-official censorship in action, this time, in advertising.

A Swedish Sjömansbiffgryta

Who hasn't been annoyed at times by certain advertisements. Usually, I suppose, we tend to ignore them or go off to make the tea while they're showing but sometimes, for good or ill, they catch our attention. The ones that annoy me particularly are what I call the 'idiot male' ads, the ones showing just how brutishly incompetent men are unless rescued by some smug, superior female ('This is how you mop up a spill on the countertop, dear') or how whiny and utterly dependent men are on some insufferably competent but resigned-to-male-stupidity female when they have a cold ('My dose id oll stuffed ub! What gan adoo?') Of course, I'm sure there are advertisements that annoy women too; indeed I'm certain we could find advertisements that annoy or upset pretty much any group you can think of. So how do we make sure that no one is ever annoyed or upset? The only completely final solution would be to ban all advertisements, except the most anodyne ones that simply say—'Get your groceries at Spendnomoney, the store that actually pays you to shop!' or the like. On the other hand, you could set up some expert group that would, on your behalf and on behalf of all other possible annoyees, determine which advertisements could be shown and which couldn't, but that's a ridiculous idea, isn't it? Alas, no, by which I mean, yes, it is a ridiculous idea but no, that hasn't prevented the Committee of Advertising Practice (CAP) from setting out a code that will once and for all get rid of all advertisements on TV, radio, posters, newspapers, magazines and billboards that, in the enlightened judgement of the Committee's members, make use of harmful or offensive stereotypes. After public consultation, the Code is expected to be in force by mid-2019. According to Ella Smillie, who takes the lead on the gender stereotyping project at the CAP, 'Our review of the evidence strongly indicates that particular forms of gender stereotypes in ads can contribute to harm for adults and children by limiting how people see themselves and how others see them and the life decisions they take.' Her co-worker, Shahriar Coupal, who is the Director of CAP, agrees with Ms Smillie. '[There] is evidence,' he said, 'that certain gender stereotypes have the potential to cause harm or serious offence ... That's why we are proposing a new rule and guidance to restrict particular gender stereotypes in ads where we believe there's an evidence-based case to do so.'

Yes, indeed. Everything I know I learned from advertisements and I am sure that your experience has been similar. Who can resist their messages, whether overt or subliminal? I am sure that there are hundreds, perhaps thousands of women and men whose lives have been moulded by the advertisements that they see, read or hear so that if those advertisements contain stereotypes, they are irrevocably forced into acting out those stereotypes in their own lives. I am sure we are all grateful to Ms Smillie and Mr Coupal and their Committee for looking after us. God only knows what we might do if she and her hard-working companions at the CAP weren't there to protect us from the appalling harms that are visited upon us by advertisements—smile, perhaps, or sigh, or get annoyed, or, who knows, turn over the page, switch to another radio or TV channel or just make the tea?

In 2018, the city of Stockholm banned sexist advertising in public spaces. The new law gives the City Council the power to remove offending images of women and men twenty four hours after they are erected. The advertisements that are banned are those that 'present women or men as simply sex objects' or 'show a stereotypical image of gender roles' or are obviously discriminatory 'in any other demeaning fashion.' The members of the Council are obviously gifted with greater powers of discernment than the average man or woman in the street. What exactly *is* it to present a man (or a woman) as simply a sex object? And now that we have perhaps as many as 200 or more genders, what exactly *is* a stereotypical image of a gender role? And how can you tell from an advertisement that it discriminates in a demeaning fashion as distinct from merely discriminating in a non-demeaning fashion or not discriminating at all but doing so in a demeaning manner?

According to the deputy Mayor of Stockholm, Daniel Helldén (Green Party—what a surprise!), the advertisements to be banned are the kind that distress many citizens. I suspect that almost every advertisement is distressing in some way or other to someone. I'm distressed by advertisements for toilet paper and sanitary products and funeral insurance and I'm sure other people have their little lists. That being so, if causing distress is the criterion for banning advertising, it's going to be difficult to have any advertising at all. But perhaps it is only certain kinds of distress that the Council has in mind. Mr Helldén explains that the advertisements to be banned are ones that affect a lot of people, 'especially younger women' and 'makes them think about their own bodies and how they look and feel in a negative way.' That this is the *raison d'être* for the censorship receives support from the reaction of one Clara Berglund to the Council's action. Ms Berglund, who is the General Secretary of the Swedish Junior Anti-Sex League—sorry, I got carried away there; that should have read 'General Secretary for the Swedish Women's Lobby'—Ms Berglund said that her organisation was happy with the Council's decision. 'We believe it's an obstacle to gender equality that people on their way to work and to school have to see these images ... It's really something that especially young women are really engaged with.'

What reasonable person could deny that young people's feeling negative about their bodies and about how they look is a Very Bad

Thing, so bad as to warrant censorship. But why this concern only with *young* people and young *female* people at that? What about those of us who are chromosomally and chronologically challenged? At my age, almost any depiction of younger and better-looking people makes me think about my own disintegrating body in an extremely negative way but the civic authorities of Dublin don't seem to be in any great hurry to relieve *my* distress. Furthermore, it might be argued that the city of Stockholm hasn't gone nearly far enough. If seeing mere images of good-looking people can cause other people such distress, especially younger women, how much more distress must they feel when they see a real live good-looking person in the streets? The City Council should consider making it illegal for good-looking young people to walk around unless their faces and figures are suitably concealed.

Kurt Vonnegut wrote the definitive treatise on this subject, cleverly disguised as a short story entitled 'Harrison Bergeron'. One passage in that treatise captures the essence of the agonising problem faced by the City Councillors of Stockholm as expressed so eloquently by Mr Helldén. George, one of Vonnegut's protagonists, is watching ballet on television. The ballerinas, he noted, 'weren't really very good—no better than anybody else would have been, anyway. They were burdened with sashweights and bags of birdshot, and their faces were masked, so that no one, seeing a free and graceful gesture or a pretty face, would feel like something the cat drug in.' (Vonnegut) Who wants to feel like something the cat drug in? In a well-ordered society, as the sapient City Councillors of Stockholm have grasped, no one should have to feel this way. So what should we do? Vonnegut, again cleverly disguising his recommendations as comic fiction, tells us. What we need, it seems, is equality, absolute equality, everywhere and in every respect. 'The year was 2018,' he writes, 'and everybody was finally equal. They weren't only equal before God and the law. They were equal every which way. Nobody was smarter than anybody else. Nobody was better looking than anybody else. Nobody was stronger or quicker than anybody else. All this equality was due to the 211th, 212th, and 213th Amendments to the Constitution, and to the unceasing vigilance of agents of the United States Handicapper General.' (Vonnegut) So have the courage of your convictions, O Councillors of Stockholm, and keep going with your essential work, no matter how much you may incur the censure of benighted reactionaries for what they see as your censorship and your sheer bloody-minded busybodiness.

Free Speech in the USA

Before we move on to consider the fraught topics of hate speech and hate crime, let's take a quick look at how the issue of free speech is handled in the USA. The United States is lucky to have the First Amendment which states, 'Congress shall make no law … abridging the freedom of speech …' This amendment, whatever its limitations, provides something of a bulwark against the Establishment's wish to curtail the speech of the man and woman in the street. But even in the USA, free speech is under threat, not only from state or national laws but also from employers (think Google) and especially on the campuses of American universities.

In a *New York Times* piece entitled 'How Conservatives Weaponized the First Amendment', Adam Liptak gives an account of the shifting perspectives of right and left in relation to the interpretation of the First Amendment. (Liptak 2018) Broadly speaking, those on the political left have shifted their views from the liberal positions the left espoused in the 1960s to objecting to what they see as, in the memorable words of Justice Elena Kagan, 'the weaponisation of the First Amendment.' On the other hand, the political right, initially suspicious of a broad understanding of the First Amendment, have now come to favour it, not least because the US Supreme Court, as currently constituted, has interpreted that Amendment in ways that they favour. When it comes to the issue of free speech, both left and right tend to approach this subject instrumentally or consequentially, the left perhaps more than the right.

The US Courts have tended to tie themselves up in knots when it comes to the issue of free speech, not least because of a tendency to conflate speech with certain forms of action which are deemed to be 'expressive speech' so, for example, burning draft cards is deemed not to be an acceptable form of free speech because in this case, a legitimate government interest trumps free speech. I should have thought burning draft cards came into the category of action rather than speech but that shows how much I know! Is nude non-obscene dancing (is there such a thing?) expressive conduct protected by the First Amendment? Only marginally, it appears, though how close to the margin such dancing comes and how the Court knows this it is impossible to say. We can only thank God for the keen marginal eyesight of the Supreme Court Justices. Cross-burning, when targeted at individuals for the purposes of criminal intimidation would appear not to be protected by the First Amendment, whereas cross burning at a political rally might well be protected. (see *Virginia vs. Black* (2003)) I find it difficult to get my head around the idea that actions that involve no words can be construed to fall under a constitutional provision explicitly dedicated to freedom of speech.

The rise of the Internet has created its own perplexities. An anti-abortion website promoted by the American Coalition of Life Activists that posted names and addresses and photographs of abortion providers and others perceived as supporting abortion rights was deemed not to have its activities protected by the First Amendment even though the site contained no explicit threats. Because violence had taken place at abortion clinics previously, Planned Parenthood had sued the group under the Freedom of Access to Clinic Entrances [FACE] Act (1994) and the jury found that the postings constituted a 'true threat' which removed their First Amendment rights.

Another central jurisprudential idea relevant to the issue of free speech is that of the public forum. The Court has found that there are two types of public forum; a traditional public forum and a limited public forum. Limited public forums attract or permit more speech restrictions than traditional public forums. Are premises 'owned' by the government public forums? Some are, some aren't (for example, the grounds of a jail). The justification for this is close to the libertarian maxim of MHMR; 'No less so than a private owner of property, the state has the power to preserve the property under its control for the use to which it is lawfully dedicated.' Other public property deemed not to constitute a public forum includes the sidewalks outside post offices and airport terminals. Public streets, on the other hand are traditional public forums and so any restrictions must be narrowly tailored to significant government interests. So, for example, picketing of individual residences on a public street is not permitted—a lot of politicians live on public streets!

In the matter of prior restraint (pre-emptive prevention), the Court operates with the standard of 'clear and present danger' to what it deems to be legitimate government interests. In the case of *Schenck* (1919) the court supported the prevention of Mr Schenck's distribution of literature that urged the military to behave insubordinately (in the context of World War I) on the grounds that Congress had a right to prevent this substantive evil. (Where is *that* in the US Constitution?) The clear and present danger test was used again in the 1950s and extended, this time not even requiring an imminent threat (*Dennis* 1951). Subsequent developments have returned the test somewhat in the direction of *Schenck*. The emergency principle enunciated by the Supreme Court is supposed to allow the government to deny free speech only when there is a clear and present danger to the state but the history of the Supreme Court on the interpretation of this principle is far from reassuring.

The American Civil Liberties Union (ACLU), once an indefatigable supporter of free speech, is under pressure to change its position on this topic, with a sizeable minority of its own employees protesting against what they call the ACLU's 'rigid' stance in defence of the First Amendment. Something similar happened in the 1970s when the ACLU came out in defence of the Skokie Nazis. The leaders of the ACLU are adamant that their approach to free speech hasn't changed but others are not so sure. Now, the policy of the ACLU is that it will not defend the free speech rights of people who are presumed to be intent on violence. But how is this presumption to be established before they even speak? Is the ACLU now advocating prior restraint?

The arguments about free speech in the USA are usually but wrongly focused on content. We have seen the USSC tie itself in knots trying to sort things out on the basis of content but the issue is not content but property. Apart from very limited instances where speech is part of a criminal act, it's not *what* you say but *where* (on whose property) you say it. For a libertarian, you can say anything you like on your own property or on the property of others willing to allow you its use for speech purposes. And that includes websites, and newspapers, and books.

Are there laws in the USA against so-called hate speech? Some such laws have been passed but the Supreme Court has generally invalidated them. For example, in *R. A. V. vs City of St Paul*, the United States Supreme Court rejected a hate-crime ordinance for infringing constitutionally protected free speech. The Minnesota Supreme Court had held that the ordinance was limited to restricting conduct that amounted to 'fighting words' but the United States Supreme Court did not agree. Of particular value here is the principle enunciated by the Supreme Court that freedom to speak will be protected, independently of the viewpoint of the speaker. If this were not so, then the government would become the entity that determines what can and cannot be said.

❧

Hate Speech, Hate Crime and Blasphemy

It does not matter much what a man hates
provided he hates something
—Samuel Butler

Hate speech

Tell the wrong kind of joke in the UK and it could cost you £1,000! Paul Gascoigne, who played football (soccer) for England, made an onstage joke in bad taste about a security guard and ended up having to plead guilty to racially aggravated abuse. Gascoigne said he didn't intend to offend anyone but the judge wasn't having any of it. 'We live in the 21st century,' he told Gascoigne, 'grow up with it or keep your mouth closed.' This is truly an extraordinary thing for the judge to say! Who is to know in advance what jokes are and what jokes are not acceptable? The only safe policy it would seem is to say nothing—which is, presumably, the intent of the PC police and their allies in the real police.

Tell the wrong kind of joke in Canada and the result will be much the same as in the UK. French-Canadian comedian Mike Ward who made a child singer with disabilities the butt of one of his jokes was fined $25,000 in moral damages and $10,000 in punitive damages and had to pay another $7,000 to the child's mother. There isn't much doubt that the joke was in extremely bad taste but then many jokes are in bad taste. Who can tell in advance? And that's the point. Decisions such as this have a pre-emptively chilling effect on speech.

Whatever you do, please don't sing in public—it could be a criminal offence. Rape, murder, assault are all of them crimes, and to this list we must now add singing. In 2015, a Glasgow man, Scott Lamont, was heard singing the words of the Billy Boys song on a public road and got a four-month gaol sentence. Was his singing really that bad! Sentencing him, the sheriff described the words of the song as 'inflammatory' and said it could have led to horrendous violence.

It's good to know that the UK's police services have their priorities right. Perpetrators of knife crime and shoplifting and car theft and other manifestly criminal activities have to take their place in the queue behind those dangerous criminals who say rude things about other people or who sing dodgy songs in public. Saying offensive things or calling people rude names is, well, it's not nice but on a scale of actual damage, it's a lot better to call people rude names or to sing stupid songs than it is to smash someone's face in or ransack someone's home. It used to be the case that law-enforcement agencies generally adopted a reasonably sane policy in this regard using the maxim, *acta non verba*, actions, not words. Now it seems the maxim is *verba acta est*—words *are* actions.

How can merely giving offence have become a crime? I am offended ten times a day whenever I read the newspapers or listen to the radio but my being offended constantly doesn't seem to rate highly enough to warrant police action and a court appearance for my offenders. Under the laws being made and enforced by the new Puritans, offensive behaviour (as determined by them, of course) is a crime. The guardians of our new public morality appear to have had their humour glands surgically removed and are prepared to defend us (even if we don't need or want to be defended) against harm-inflicting jokes. Indeed we are blessed. Our masters are truly virtuous and we had better become virtuous too—or else!

But it's not just in the UK that you have to talk on eggshells. In Germany, you had better be especially careful of what you say. The leader of Germany's Pegida movement was convicted and fined €9,600 for calling refugees cattle, filth and scum in a 2014 Facebook post. This conviction was obtained under Germany's 'incitement to hatred' law, the *Volksverhetzung*. This law bans speech that could incite hatred against a national, racial, religious or ethnic minority. As well as limiting speech that calls for 'violent or arbitrary measures', it also regulates affronts to human dignity 'by insulting segments of the population or individuals because of their belonging to a minority group'. A YouTube blogger was sentenced to eight months in prison and fined €15,000 for referring to striking train conductors as 'vermin' who should be gassed. 'Do you remember how the Jews were brought to Auschwitz by train? That's where we should bring these conductors,' he wrote. A fine of €3,150 was imposed on a 56-year-old, who had written nasty stuff about Muslims on the internet. Two football fans were fined €5,400 each for singing a chant about building an underground line from Jerusalem to Auschwitz. I suspect that very few people (including me) would actually approve of any of these transgressions of the *Volksverhetzung* but it's clear that German lawmakers do not trust the ordinary people of Germany despite the fact that 70% of Germans are so right-thinking that they believe it is in order for the government to criminalise speech deemed offensive to minorities! If you consider that pretty much anyone is a member of some minority or other, that portends a future in which no one may say anything that might be deemed offensive about anyone but, of course, as we all know, there are minorities and then there are minorities. Not all minorities are equal; some, like the pigs in *Animal Farm*, are more equal than others.

Ursula Haverbeck, an octogenarian German granny, had an arrest warrant issued against her when she failed to show up to serve the two-and-a-half year sentence imposed on her for inciting the German people to holocaust denial. There is, to my mind, something particularly peculiar in having a crime of inciting people to hold beliefs but let us put that radical thought to one side for a moment. What a dangerous woman Frau Haverbeck must be! The sentence was imposed on her in August 2017 when she lost her appeal to reverse an earlier ten-month sentence she had received. Germany's highest court ruled that denying the mass murder of Jews during Nazi Germany is not covered by the right to free speech. The judges were of the opinion that 'The dissemination of untrue and deliberately false statements of fact can not contribute to the development of public opinion and thus do not fall within the remit of protection for free speech.' Furthermore, 'the denial of the Nazi genocide goes beyond the limits of the peacefulness of public debate and threatens public peace.' Frau Haverbeck was later arrested at her home in Vlotho and finally began to serve her sentence. I'm sure all right-thinking Germans breathed a sigh of relief that this dangerous felon was finally behind bars!

The *Volksverhetzung* is often justified as necessary for protecting minorities from the fury of the masses but the primary function of this kind of law is to send a strong pre-emptive signal to all Germans to watch what they say. As one might expect, similar laws exist in other jurisdictions. In Ireland, we have the Prohibition of Incitement to Hatred Act; in the UK, the Public Order Act 1986 which makes it a criminal offence to incite ethnic or racial hatred; and in Sweden and Finland agitation against an ethnic group is prohibited by the criminal code. Welcome to the wonderful world of hate speech and its companion in iniquity, hate-crime.

I began this book by recounting the sad fate of Mark Meechan (aka Count Dankula) and his (or, rather, his girlfriend's) Nazi-Saluting Pug. Commenting on Meechan's fate, Alexander Adams says,

> The conviction of Mark Meechan is the result of this same identity politics, political monoculture and virtue-signalling of the ruling class. This situation is no good for anyone. In fact, the existence of classes protected by the ruling elite only builds resentment that actually damages those protected groups. They become the subject of ire because our very sense of fairness rebels at the idea of certain groups becoming specially advantaged. But it is not too late to defuse this situation. We must begin to treat all people fairly, and according to their actions. We must abolish hate-speech laws, and stop travelling down the road to censorship. (Adams 2018)

The argument that speech laws, however well intentioned (and they may not always be well-intentioned) can actually be counter-productive is also made by Nadine Strossen who points out in her splendid book *Hate, Why We Should Resist It with Free Speech, not Censorship* that hate-speech laws can end up targeting the very minority groups such laws purport to protect. 'In 2010,' she writes, 'Amnesty International and Reporters Without Borders complained that in Kyrgyzstan a prominent journalist who is a member of the Uzbek minority, and the Uzbek newspaper he edited, were baselessly charged with "inciting ethnic hatred" due to their reporting on conflicts between Uzbeks and the Majority Kyrgyz.' (Strossen 2018, 86) A knife will cut the hand of the guilty and innocent alike.

One problem with criminalising hate speech is that in contemporary society what constitutes hatred is a moveable feast. If one says that homosexual actions are intrinsically sinful, one could find oneself charged with a hate speech crime. A Swedish pastor received a one-month suspended prison sentence for saying that homosexuality is a tumour on society. You may not believe that homosexuality is a tumour on society but he does and he was punished for his beliefs. Do you think that men are men and women women? I think so and perhaps you do too but if you say this you may very well be guilty of being transphobic and of expressing hatred of trans people? Do you think that the idea of same-sex marriage is spectacularly and self-evidently stupid? That's pretty much guaranteed to be regarded as homophobic. If you express the hope in public that your least favourite politician would shuffle off this mortal coil, is this (admittedly uncharitable) hope a credible death threat? What can you say online without expecting a visit from the old Bill? It's not entirely clear, and as with all unclear situations, people will censor themselves, rather than risk ending up on the end of a criminal charge.

What's hate speech to you may be someone else's genuine moral conviction. In April 2019, the Australian rugby player, Israel Folau, said in a social media post that gay people would go to hell if they didn't repent. Folau might be correct in his theological opinions or he might not but he seems to have fallen victim to the 'You can't say that!' culture. Rugby Australia, with which Folau signed a multi-million dollar contract in February, said that Folau would be sacked if there weren't what they termed 'compelling mitigating factors' that would justify the post. Australia's opposition leader remarked. 'There is no freedom to perpetuate hateful speech,' and New Zealand's prime minister commented, somewhat more vaguely, '[Folau is] a person in a position of influence and I think that with that comes responsibility ... I'm particularly mindful of young people who are members of our rainbow community, there is a lot of vulnerability there.'

Other commentators were somewhat more reluctant to, ahem, put the boot into Folau for his theological opinions, with the former coach of Australia's rugby team, Alan Jones, going so far as to say that Rugby Australia's decision 'endangered free speech in Australia' and that it 'had been driven by RA's concern not to upset sponsors.' 'It has,' he said, 'nothing to do with Israel [Folau], or rugby, or religion, homosexuals, or whatever. Where are we in this country on free speech?' (see Newman 2019)

If Folau had posted that adulterers or drunkards would go to hell if they didn't repent, I wonder if Australia's opposition leader would have been moved to condemn this as hate speech, or New Zealand's prime minister to worry about vulnerable young members of the adulterers' or drunkards' community. Wait a minute! Folau *did* include adulterers and drunkards, as well as thieves, atheists, idolaters and liars in his list of those who are destined for hell unless they repent. Here's what he wrote: 'Warning. Drunks, homosexuals, adulterers, liars, fornicators, thieves, atheists, idolaters. Hell awaits you. Repent! Only Jesus saves.' I am waiting with bated breath to see a media backlash or the Twitter mob describing him as an adultero-phobe or a drunkardophobe!

The Australian journalist Crispin Hull was one of the few to point out the obvious fact that the issue here is not really whether what Folau said is theologically correct or not but whether in Australia today there is or there is not freedom of speech. According to Hull, Rugby Australia's treatment of Folau is 'mired in hypocrisy' inasmuch as, though it calls itself an 'inclusive organisation', its inclusive policy doesn't seem to include fundamentalist Christians. He goes on to wonder what Rugby Australia would do if confronted with a tweet by a Muslim player that pointed out that Allah takes a dim view of drunks, liars, fornicators and homosexuals.

Why should it be assumed that what Folau wrote was, in fact, an example of *hate* speech? Perhaps it could better be taken as an example of *love* speech, a friendly and charitable warning addressed to those in moral or spiritual danger, much as one might warn those with a propensity for walking on cliff edges of the perils to life and limb that such an activity entails. Hull points out that there is, in fact, nothing necessarily hateful about Folau's tweet, remarking that 'Folau—however misguided—had the interests of homosexuals and atheists and others at heart. In his Christian world, he was trying to help them avoid the horrors of the eternal hellfire.' (Hull 2019) When Folau was finally fired in May 2019, the chief executive of

Rugby Australia, Raelene Castle, commented, apparently without any sense of irony, 'Rugby Australia fully supports [players'] right to their own beliefs ... When we say rugby is a game for all, we mean it. People need to feel safe and welcomed in our game regardless of their gender, race, background, religion, or sexuality.' Ms Castle's 'all' doesn't seem to include fundamentalist Christians who express their beliefs publicly. I wonder just how safe and welcomed by Rugby Australia Israel Folau feels?

If you can't express your biases or your hatreds or what others perceive as your biases or hatreds, then you've been pre-emptively gagged. You are at the mercy of those who get to determine what is and what isn't hate speech where hate speech is simply whatever those who are given to censorship and have the power to censor find hateful! But speech which is merely offensive to certain individuals groups (as distinct from violating the ZAP) should not be censored by legal means and the very existence of hate-speech laws implicitly denies that there are ways, non-legal but effective ways, of regulating speech, insinuating that, without legal prohibition, there would be no constraints on what can and cannot be said. But societies have always regulated speech informally through social sanctions even if, as Mill suspected, some of these modes of regulation might themselves approach the borderlands of tyranny.

When it comes right down to it, isn't hate speech just an aspect (an unpleasant aspect to be sure) of free speech? Not according to the EU Commissioner for Justice, Consumers and Gender Equality, Vera Jourová. 'Illegal hate speech online is not only a crime,' she says, 'it represents a threat to free speech and democratic engagement ... In May 2016, I initiated the Code of conduct on online hate speech, because we urgently needed to do something about this phenomenon. Today, after two and a half years, we can say that we found the right approach and established a standard throughout Europe on how to tackle this serious issue, while fully protecting freedom of speech.' (European Commission 2019) Tanya Cohen, a feminist commentator, agrees, with Jourová. She thinks that the United States needs to 'get tough on hate speech through the law'. 'I am,' Ms Cohen bravely confesses, 'a strong believer in the unalienable right to freedom of speech' and who can doubt her for, after all, she deprecates the prohibition of certain forms of unpopular speech such as 'pro-LGBT speech in Russia'. But, she warns us not to make the mistake of confusing hate speech with free speech. Hate speech is speech that 'offends or insults in general, along with speech that voices approval of anti-democratic, anti-freedom, and/or totalitarian ideologies and propaganda for war'. Ms Cohen is not quite so keen to protect this form of speech. Ms Cohen then, it appears, is a strong supporter of free speech—except, of course, when she isn't.

Hate is an emotion and not a particularly attractive one. It is and should be the object of moral and spiritual evaluation but hate just by itself has never been, until now, a matter for the law. If I sit in my study hating all sorts of people and objects and groups and actions with an all-encompassing and virulent hatred, I may thereby cause some moral or spiritual damage to myself but as long as I sit in my room and do not act on my hatreds, no one else is harmed. Hate which expresses itself in speech also does no harm to others unless it is a credible threat to their persons or property. Hate, then, just by itself isn't and shouldn't be a crime. You can hate just about anyone or anything you like and the law should not be able to touch you.

That being the case, what *is* a hate crime? It appears to be an offence that would be an offence even without the hate—assault or vandalism, for example—but where the motivation for the offence is the hatred of a specific category of victim. A slew of hate-speech laws and non-discrimination laws has given legal firepower to those seeking the repression of free speech. Even if such laws are not actively deployed, an atmosphere of political correctness allied to the baying Twitter mob is often enough to eradicate dissent. Many cases before the courts involve Christians not wishing to act in ways that they believe endorse, condone, or celebrate same-sex marriage or other violations of their religious consciences. In the UK, a Christian marriage registrar, a Christian guest-house owner, a Christian printer and others have been forced to choose between their consciences and their livelihoods and then there was the test case of Asher's Bakery, of which, more later. But the coercive conformity we see is by no means limited to religion. For every public or political issue there is now a 'right' and a 'wrong' view, and if you're in the wrong, civil disagreement is becoming increasingly impossible. If you hold the wrong views, you are a bigot, on the wrong side of history, and you *must* be punished.

Hate crime

The UK's London Metropolitan Police (the Met) defines a hate crime, in a preliminary way, as the commission of a crime against a person because of that person's disability, gender identity, race, sexual orientation, religion, or any other perceived difference. That's fairly broad! *Any* other perceived difference? Perceived difference between what and what? According to the Met, hate crime doesn't have to include physical violence. The use of offensive language by you towards another person or harassing them because of who they are or who you think they are, is a crime. Posting abusive or offensive messages about people online may also be a hate crime. Speaking somewhat more strictly, the Met defines a hate crime as any criminal offence 'which is perceived by the victim or any other person to be motivated by hostility or prejudice based on a person's race or perceived race; religion or perceived religion; sexual orientation or perceived sexual orientation; disability or perceived disability and any crime motivated by hostility or prejudice against a person who is transgender or perceived to be transgender.'

There are a number of interesting facets to this definition. First, the offence must already be criminal even without the element of hate. Second, it need only be *perceived* by someone, not necessarily the victim, as being motivated by hostility or prejudice, it doesn't actually have to *be* so motivated. The Met tell us that in fact evidence of the hate elements isn't even a requirement! Third, the hostility or prejudice must be based on the victim's real or perceived race, religion, sexual orientation, disability or transgender status. Unlike the Met's preliminary definition, there is no mention of other differences, such as age, political beliefs, height, weight, body shape, clothing (and so on) all of which could conceivably, if not reasonably, be the object of someone's hostility or prejudice. Hate crime involves hostility or prejudice against people because they are members of certain groups but why *these* groups and not others? Why is one victim's suffering as the result of a crime worthy of more punishment to the aggressor than another's?

Hate *crime* laws are conceptually distinct from laws against hate *speech*. Whereas hate speech laws criminalise a category of speech, hate crime laws increase the penalties for conduct that is already criminal under other laws. If the concept of hate speech is hateful; so too is the concept of hate-crime legislation, which is a fairly transparent attempt to control speech and, with it, thought. In some respects, the notion of hate crime is another manifestation of the triumph of feelings over reason. Hurt feelings now appear to matter as much, if not more, than goods stolen or bones broken. In another triumph for the ascendancy of feelings over objectivity, the judge of whether or not a hate crime has occurred is the putative victim. But just as no politician or political party can be found to call the apparent generosity of minimum-wage legislation into question for to do so would be to appear hard-hearted and uncaring, so too, no politician or political party can be found to question the idiocy of hate-crime legislation lest they be thought to approve of hateful speech or crime.

Even if it is shown that certain forms of speech cause harm, that is not sufficient to justify prohibiting them. It all depends upon what you mean by harm. Some harm is entirely defensible, for example, taking the last cucumber sandwich (à la *The Importance of Being Earnest*) or getting a job which means that all the other candidates are harmed by your so doing (that is, they didn't get the job). On the other hand, some harms are not defensible, such as stabbing a rival football supporter to death because he disrespected your football team.

There are two reasons to permit or to prohibit X. One reason is principled: X is right and so should be permitted or X is wrong and so should be prohibited. The other reason is consequential: if X is permitted, it will have good results; if is not prohibited, it will have bad results. It's not clear, on a consequential level, that hate speech laws actually achieve what they set out to achieve. But the efficacy of consequential reasons to one side, the basis on which this issue should be decided is not in the end consequential but principled.

The crime of incitement to hatred is defined as someone's acting in a way that is threatening and intended to stir up hatred. If someone acts in a threatening manner, that would seem to correspond to the old category of assault in which a potential victim entertains a reasonable expectation of battery to come. A drunk comes up to you late at night on the street and, shaking his fist close to your face, says, 'I'm going to punch your lights out!' In those circumstances, you might reasonably fear that battery is about to follow. So far, so good. But incitement to hatred doesn't just include threatening behaviour but the intention to stir up hatred and it's far from obvious why *that* should be legally problematic.

Hate crime laws can be found in many countries and their provisions are, in the main, very similar. For example, Armenia increases the penalties for crimes committed by persons acting from ethnic, racial or religious motives. In France, you'll get 30 years for plain murder, but a life sentence if it's murder motivated by hate. In Germany, you won't find hate crime legislation as such but you will find that speech is criminalised under a number of different laws. Section 46 of the Criminal Code allows sentencing to take account of, *inter alia*, the motives of the criminal. The categories of possible victims in Belgium is significantly wider than in many other countries. The usual suspects are found, to be sure, but also included are birth, fortune, age, religious or philosophical beliefs, current or future states of health, handicaps or physical features.

'Hate is hate', proclaims the title of an article written by Alison Saunders, the 2017 UK Director of Public Prosecutions, explaining the UK's Crown Prosecution Service's (CPS) guidelines on hate crime on social media. (Saunders 2017) Thank you, Ms Saunders, I'm sure we are all a lot clearer on this topic now, especially those of us who might have been predisposed to think that hate is joy or love or rapture. Hate is indeed hate—and fear is fear, and jealousy is jealousy, and cream doughnuts are cream doughnuts, and men are men, and women are women and.....oh no, wait—I forgot, some men are women and some women are men; ignore the last couple of illustrations. The statement X is X is invariably true and equally invariably unhelpful to any reasoned discussion. What is intended by such seemingly vacuous statements is not really 'Hate is hate' but rather, 'Whatever I shall deem to be hate(ful speech/writing) shall be that and shall be subject to criminal sanctions and I don't want to hear any backchat about it.'

Abusive or offensive messages on social media can now be classified as hate crimes, and the perpetrators subjected to harsh sentencing. When it comes to verbal abuse, the Met tells us that such abuse 'can be a common and extremely unpleasant experience for minority groups'. That is no doubt true, but would it not be an unpleasant experience for *any* group, even a non-minority group. What if you're white, male and heterosexual and someone abuses you verbally or calls you names *because* you are a white, male, heterosexual. Isn't that problematic at all? A statement on the CPS website said that, 'in recognition of the growth of hate crime perpetrated using social media', the CPS will 'treat online crime as seriously as offline offences, while taking into account the potential impact on the wider community as well as the victim'. Saunders claimed that there were 15,000 hate-crime prosecutions between 2015 and 2016, clearly not enough to satisfy the CPS which is trying to drum up business by using a social-media campaign to encourage more people to report offensive posts.

According to the CPS, a hate crime 'can include verbal abuse, intimidation, threats, harassment, assault and bullying, as well as damage to property'. As we've seen, the official definition includes an essential reference to the crime's motivation by either hostility or prejudice. What constitutes 'hostility'? Well, the CPS says it uses the 'everyday understanding of the word', which can include 'ill-will, spite, contempt, prejudice, unfriendliness, antagonism, resentment and dislike'. Ill-will, spite, contempt are, no doubt, moral failings but I've yet to see a reasoned case to establish why the manifestation of such moral failings should be taken to be crimes or why crimes motivated by such moral failings should occupy a special position in the gallery of criminal law as distinct from greed crimes or jealously crimes or envy crimes or any other crimes that might be motivated by moral failings other than hate or hostility.

It's foolish to equate online posts with personal interactions. Tweeting something unpleasant to or about someone is not the same thing as shouting abuse at a person in the street, and neither of them is at the same level with actual battery. Ms Saunders, however, writes 'We should remember that there is a less visible frontline which is easily accessible to those in the UK who hold extreme views on race, religion, sexuality, gender and even disability. I refer to the online world where an increasing proportion of hate crime is now perpetrated'. Saunders is worried about the proliferation of what she calls 'extreme views' and their airing on social media. 'People all over the world,' she says, 'are questioning how those in positions of power can counter the kinds of extreme views that are increasingly being aired, and how societies might do more to prevent such opinions from gestating in the first place'.

The policing and punishment of hate crime

Are fears of a police-stateish approach to online speech exaggerated? Not if the story of Harry Miller's 'like' is to be believed. In early 2019, Miller re-tweeted a limerick which expressed scepticism about whether transgender women were biological women. This limerick, which won't win any poetry prizes, included the inspired and immortal lines, 'Your breasts are made of silicone, your vagina goes nowhere.' Miller was contacted by a Police Constable, Mansoor Gul, who told him that his re-tweet would be recorded as a hate incident. He also said to Miller, as one speaking *de haut en bas*, 'I've been on a course and what you need to understand is that you can have a foetus with a female brain that grows male body parts and that's what a transgender person is.' Those of us who haven't been fortunate enough to take that course are now wised up. PC Gul confirmed that he had spoken to Mr Miller. He said, 'Although none of the tweets were criminal, I said to Mr Miller that the limerick is the kind of thing that upsets the transgender community. I warned him that if it escalates we will have to take further action.'

Is seems PC Gul was following up a complaint. The complainant had managed to identify Mr Miller's place of work even though there was no reference to his business on his Twitter account and alleged that the firm was an 'unsafe environment' for transgender employees because of Mr Miller's social media comments. At one point, PC

Gul referred to the complainant as a 'victim' and when Mr Miller wonder how there could be a victim if there had been no crime, PC Gul informed him, 'We need to check your thinking.' It's good to know that the Humberside police force have their priorities straight and that checking people's thinking appears to be somewhat more important than reducing the number of violent offences (up 24%), sexual offences (up 19%) and robberies (up 17%). Miller says that since he described the incident on Twitter, he has received many messages from people who are terrified of speaking out on transgender issues in case of police action. With people like PC Gul on the job, I'm not surprised they are terrified!

In Florida in 2016, Michael Wolfe broke into a mosque in Titusville and there left a slab of raw bacon. For this crime, Wolfe will serve 15 years in state prison, followed by 15 years on probation. It should be conceded that Wolfe has a criminal record for burglary and grand theft but what made his vandalising the mosque really serious wasn't so much the criminal damage he inflicted on the building but what is called the 'hate crime enhancement' which turned his actions into a felony.

It seems, however, that not all hate is equally worthy of legal reprobation. In stark contrast to the severity of Wolfe's sentence for bacon-baiting, three Palestinians who attempted to burn a synagogue in Wuppertal in Germany in 2014 were effectively given a judicial slap on the wrist when the authorities considering their case concluded that their attempted arson wasn't an anti-Semitic act but merely some criticism of Israel that had simply gone too far! In another incident, in December 2017, 3,000 Muslims outside the US embassy in London chanted the anti-Semitic cry; *'Khaybar Khaybar, ya yahud, Jaish Muhammad, sa yahud'* or 'Jews, remember Khaybar the army of Muhammad is returning'. Jewish human rights groups, considering the chant to be an incitement to violence against Jewish people, appealed to the Metropolitan Police to take action following the anti-semitic chanting, but it doesn't seem that any investigation has yet been undertaken.

By contrast to these cases of apparent anti-Semitism, take the case of Richard Evans. What was his crime? On Facebook, Evans, who is the son of the owner of the company that hired a van to Darren Osborne, the man who drove it into a group of Muslims outside Finsbury Park Mosque in June 2017, wrote, ' … it's a shame they don't hire out steam rollers or tanks could have done a tidy job then.' Not a nice thing to say. One might even think it both gross and stupid. But Mr Evans was arrested 'on suspicion of displaying threatening, abusive, insulting written material with intent that is likely to stir up racial hatred'. Racial hatred, eh? What race would that be, then? I was under the impression that Islam was a religion not a race but perhaps I was mistaken. Putting to one side the odd mention of race in this connection, do the authorities really think that it's their role to arrest people who make stupid or nasty comments online? The answer, sadly, appears to be—yes. Their view of the plain people of Britain is, apparently, that they are sitting, zombie-like, in front of their computers just waiting to be encouraged to hate people on the basis of their race. 'See,' they say to one another, 'some nobody has said something nasty about Muslims. Let's go hate them all. Or rather, let's not just hate them, but let's do something terrible to them.'

In late 2017, a man was jailed in the UK for a year for writing a Facebook post. The message, posted after the Manchester terror attack, included the phrase 'Let's kill every Muslim'. Was this an incitement to violence? Was it the beginning of a joint action that would lead to the death of every Muslim? Even the Crown Prosecution Service conceded that no harmful action was attributable to the post. The charge was one of publishing material with the intention of stirring up religious hatred. One can immediately grant that what was written was not pleasant, not nice, not clever, not a lot of things, including, realistically, not an incitement to violence. Given the context, it reads like a hyperbolic emotional outburst, mere speech, nasty speech without a doubt, but mere speech nonetheless, not the beginning of a criminal action such as conspiracy or attempt.

Stuart Taylor, writing in *The Atlantic* (May 2007) puts some criminal cases before us for consideration. The first case, which concerns events that really happened, is that of Christopher Newsom and Channon Christian who had their car hijacked and were raped (he as well as she), tortured and then killed. The victims and their assailants were members of different races. The other case (hypothetical) concerns Sam who knocks into Martin in a crowded bar, spilling beer on Martin's sweatshirt which has 'Gay pride' emblazoned on it. Martin is not pleased and shouts at Sam, 'You stupid bastard, I should kick your ass' to which Sam replies, 'You damned queer' and punches Martin in the face, splitting his lip. Which of these two events displays a hate crime? Well, according to the relevant criteria, the second would probably qualify as a hate crime as Sam would seem to harbour a hatred for homosexuals. What of the first? Probably not, because even though the rapists and murderers of the young couple were undoubtedly full of hate and were of a different race from the victims, it can't be definitely established that they did it *because* they hated their victims' race. By the way, in the real case, the victims were white and those charged with the crime were black.

Section 18C of Australia's *Racial Discrimination Act* makes it unlawful to 'offend, insult, humiliate or intimidate a person because of their race or ethnicity'. It is manifestly a multicultural monstrosity and should be repealed forthwith but, in the interim, if it is to be applied at all, it should be applied to everyone. And that includes the University of Melbourne's little piece of dance theatre entitled 'Where We Stand' which, according to the *Australian* newspaper, sees members of the audience segregated by the colour of their skin and ritually humiliated and intimidated to the point of harassment because of their race. According to a leading article in the *Spectator*, one 'clearly distraught elderly woman who had come to see a granddaughter perform ... was racially harangued by four female 'dancers' in the lobby and forced to sign a political treatise before being allowed into the show. Upon admittance, the dance performance was stopped deliberately, in order to further humiliate those white people who had just entered.' (Anon 2018) It's hard to see how this nonsense doesn't fall under section 18C unless, of course, there are different strokes for different folks.

Why is there a category of 'hate crime'?

Why did the category of hate crime spring into existence? Was it because there were large gaps in the criminal law that needed to be filled or was it that some of our more awful criminals couldn't otherwise be adequately punished? It must be conceded, I believe, that the notion of 'hate crime' is largely symbolic and is intended to send a message of support to the members of certain groups which, it is believed, are especially at risk from criminals. Reporting on CNN in October 2018, Eric Levenson asks why hate crimes matter and his answer to his own question is that 'The idea is to show the targeted community—people of that race, religion, disability, ethnicity, gender, sexual orientation or gender identity—that their lives and identities matter.' A hate crime is a crime committed against Tom, Dick or Harriet not in their capacities as individual human beings but as members or representatives of certain groups conceived to be specially-at-risk. Hate crime law, then, in punishing the thoughts of criminals does so insofar as those thoughts are directed negatively (by means of hatred or prejudice) against certain identifiable groups and so such laws are a particularly insidious manifestation of identity politics.

In their excellent *Criminal Law and Identity Politics* (1998), James Jacobs and Kimberly Potter, having characterised hate crime as an attempt to eliminate prejudice in society by the use of the criminal law, raise some significant points that must be seriously considered. First, how do we define the prejudices that the hate crime laws are intended to eliminate? Second, why *these* prejudices and not others? Why racism, for example, but not ageism or disabledism? Why not have attempts to stamp out prejudice against people who speak with a Birmingham accent or people who have red hair or people who are politically conservative? (I had just written the foregoing sentence which was intended as a mild form of *reductio ad absurdum* when the *Telegraph* reported that the UK's then Home Secretary Sajid Javid had asked the Law Commission to investigate whether or not ageism and misogyny should be covered by the hate crime umbrella! It seems that 'one million older people are victims of physical, financial, psychological and sexual abuse each year yet ... convictions are rare and sentences too lenient.' (Hymas 2019) It is hard to argue by *reductio ad absurdum* when the absurd becomes the new normal!)

Stella Creasy MP wants to add misogyny to the list of hates that already aggravate offences while Mr Javid has also asked the Law Commission to consider whether misandry should be added to the ever-expanding list of hate crimes. This has provoked some resistance from members of the already well-established beneficiaries of hate crime laws. Gaby Hinsliff tells us that 'the test for misandry to join the list would be the same as for any other form of hate: is there evidence of a serious problem with men being stalked, beaten up by strangers on the street, having bricks chucked through their windows or being otherwise persecuted by women motivated by dislike or contempt for men in general? If so, then misandrist hate crime must be acknowledged in law and rooted out.' (Hinsliff 2018) I think it's fairly clear from this passage that Ms Hinsliff is sceptical about whether this is or there can be such a thing as misandry. I share her doubts as to whether misandry should be added to the list of hate crimes but that's because I doubt that there should be any such list to begin with. If this expansion of groups supposedly protected by hate crime laws continues, it will eventually cover every eventuality. When every crime becomes a hate crime, then the distinction loses all point, not that it had much to begin with.

Since hate-crimes laws are directed at those who, by definition, are criminals, or are likely to be criminals, what reason have we, ask Jacobs & Potter, to think that they will be moved to become equal opportunity offenders by such laws? 'It would take some heroic assumptions,' they write, 'to believe that bigoted and anti-social criminals and potential criminals, if they are listening at all, will be any more responsive to this message than they have been to all the other threats and condemnations contained in criminal laws that they regularly ignore.' (Jacobs & Potter, 68)

Hate crimes, then, in addition to involving the criminalisation of thought, are essentially political in origin and in effect. They are demanded by a variety of victim groups for symbolic reasons (recognition of their special victim status and the pre-emptive repression of criticism) and for material reasons (allocation of funding and legal resources) and they are provided by politicians for, as one would expect, political reasons, not least among which is the attractive and cost-free benefit (cost-free to the politician if not to society at large) of signalling one's superior virtues.

Writing in the *Telegraph* in October 2018, the UK's Home Secretary, Sajid Javid, told us that 'Hate crime has no place in Britain, and now the Government has vowed to stamp out such behaviour' and he announced more support for the victims of hate crimes, including the provision of 'extra funding for community groups and educational organisations, and works to promote shared values. We will be giving nearly £800,000 to religious institutions so they can upgrade their security through the Places of Worship scheme, which has helped protect churches, mosques, Hindu temples and Sikh Gurdwaras. This brings funding through the scheme to around £1.5 million.' (Javid)

The passing of hate crime laws tells the lobbyists for the various victim groups, that politicians are on their side. Jacobs and Potter go so far as to say that '...the primary purpose of hate crime laws is to bolster the morale and strategic position of certain identity groups, not to impose heavier sanctions on prejudiced offenders.' (Jacobs & Potter, 73-4) Just as the policies of affirmative action and gender-quotas paradoxically institutionalise and reinforce the very divisions in society that they are allegedly intended to eliminate, so too, hate crime laws implant considerations of race and sex and sexual orientation and religion firmly into the heart of public policy-making and law-making. That being so, it's not obvious that delineating sections of the population as permanent victims who have a claim to special consideration and treatment will promote the idea that justice is and ought to be blind.

Jacobs and Potter conclude, 'The concepts of prejudice and bigotry are political to the core. Hate crime laws explicitly seek to punish people for having bigoted beliefs ... It would appear that the only additional purpose in punishing more severely those who commit a bias crime is to provide extra punishment based on the offender's politically incorrect opinions and viewpoints.' (Jacobs & Potter, 127-8)

Perhaps it might be argued that the category of hate crime is justified because its object is not just the protection of the particular victim of a particular crime but the entire group of which the victim is somehow taken to be a representative. Expressing this point, the Oregon Supreme Court held that hate crime 'creates a harm to society distinct from and greater than the harm caused by the assault alone. Such crimes—because they are directed not only toward the victim but, in essence, toward an entire group of which the victim is perceived to be a member—invite imitation, retaliation, and insecurity on the part of persons in the group to which the victim was perceived by the assailants to belong.' (cited in Jacobs & Potter, 86)

As should be obvious, hate crimes are not unique in this respect. Burglaries in a given neighbourhood, for example, have been known to heighten fears among the adjacent non-burgled property owners that they may be in line for attack. To generalise the argument, it seems to depend upon the idea that hate crimes warrant more severe sentences than non-hate crimes because third-parties will be disturbed by them in some special way. But then the question arises: is the possibility that third parties will be disturbed by such crimes a justification for allocating stiffer sentences to them? Jacobs and Potter ask us to consider a case where a judge might enhance 'the punishment of a black defendant who robbed a white victim on the ground that fear of black robbers was creating deep anxiety and terror in the white community, leading to white flight from the city, and to the deterioration of the city's tax base?' If you would not be prepared to countenance such a judicial sentencing practice in this case, on what grounds would you justify it were the races to be reversed?

Greed and other reprehensible motives

On April 1st, 2019, Dublin was the scene of a spectacular crime caper. In what Gardaí [the Irish police force] described as the 'crime of the mid-morning tea break', 24 cream doughnuts were brazenly stolen from a city-centre patisserie. The Gardaí followed a trail of doughnut crumbs to a remote location and arrested a suspect who was named as Billy Bunter, a pupil of the South Dublin school, Greyfriars. When arrested and charged, Bunter was unable to make a statement as his mouth was full of doughnut but he had cream all over his face and doughnut crumbs scattered over his clothes. The arresting officer perceived this crime to be motivated by greed so Bunter will be charged not just with theft but with a 'greed' crime, which attracts a higher punishment tariff. A greed crime is defined as any incident which is perceived as being motivated by greed by the victim or by any other person and which is based on an inordinate desire for food, drink, money, clothes, electronic equipment, or anything else that might be inordinately desired by anyone.

Sounds ridiculous? Well, then, how about *this* piece of proposed legislation? In 2001, a bill was introduced in Portland, Oregon that called for an additional five years in prison for miscreants whose crime was motivated by hatred of people who subscribe to beliefs that support capitalism or those whose crime consisted of violently supporting the downgrading of the needs of human beings to protect the unspoiled nature of the environment. According to the local press, the target of the (admittedly) novel legislation were eco-terrorists and critics of capitalism. Senator Gary George who sponsored the bill may have had his tongue firmly in his cheek but his point is a serious one; why is a crime that is motivated by hatred of one set of aspects of human life to be punished with additional severity but not crimes that are motivated by hatred of other aspects of human life?

This raises some serious questions. Is a criminal's motive relevant to the determination of whether or not a crime has been committed? If it is not relevant to the determination of the crime, why should it be relevant when it comes to the allocation of punishment? If I were to steal the Crown Jewels, my intention in so doing is to assume the rights of an owner with respect to that set of sparklers. My motive might be my own enrichment or it might be the endowment of a hospital in Africa for those suffering from some dreadful but curable disease. Similarly, Robin Hood's motive might have been the lightening of the burdens of the Nottinghamshire poor but his intention was to remove what he stole from the control of the Sheriff of Nottingham and to assume control of it himself.

To those (like me) who argue that taking motivation into account is, or should be, irrelevant to determining the nature of a crime it might be responded—'well, mental elements are already relevant in, for example, homicide, to determine the difference between murder and manslaughter. To be convicted of murder, the accused must have intended to kill or cause serious harm to the victim. So there can't be any principled objection to including mental elements as part of a crime.' There is a significant difference, however. In murder, the relevant mental element is the *intention* to kill or cause serious bodily harm. The *motivation* for that intention, also a mental element, whether hatred or greed or callousness, is irrelevant to the determination of the character of the crime. It may be relevant in helping to discover the criminal but that's a different matter. In hate crime, so-called, the *intention* is to cause harm of some kind to the victim. The *motivation* for the harm inflicted on the victim is perceived to be hatred and, unlike the case of murder, is taken to be partially constitutive of the crime itself.

So, the pertinent mental element in crime should be the intention of the criminal, not his motive. If John Boyne Crippen killed Cora Crippen and intended to kill her or to cause her serious bodily harm, he is guilty of murder. If he did this out of hate or any other negative emotion, while that affects the *moral* dimension of his act, it doesn't affect its *legal* quality. It doesn't make it a 'hate crime', any more than greed would make it a 'greed crime'.

	Hate crime	Murder
Intention	to cause harm of some kind	to kill or cause serious bodily harm
Motivation	hatred—partially constitutive of the nature of the crime. Here, the *why* of the crime has become part of the *what* of the crime.	hatred—perhaps relevant to discovering the identity of the killer but irrelevant to the determination of the nature of the crime. What is relevant is *what* the killer intended to do, not *why* he intended to do it.

Motive may be understood as the psychological element that provides the explanatory context for the intention that is constitutive of the criminal act. Consider the following two cases. Suppose I want to be rich so that I can live a lavish lifestyle but, unfortunately, I have a rooted aversion to work and I chose the wrong parents (parents with no money). But there is lots of money in my local bank so I carry out a robbery to get the money I want. On the other hand, suppose I am appalled by the ravages caused by disease in Africa, much of which could be alleviated by money. I have no money so I rob a bank to get the money to send to Africa. In both cases, the intention is to convert the assets of the bank to my own purposes, assuming the rights of an owner towards them. In both cases, I have engaged in an act of theft. But the motives of the two cases differ significantly and while this affects the moral character of the acts, it doesn't affect their legal character.

Hateful thoughts are not crimes. Neither is hate speech. Hate action may be a crime but only if the action, whether accompanied by hate or not, is already a crime. *Why* a crime is committed may be relevant to its investigation and detection but it is irrelevant to *whether* or not a crime has been committed. If someone bashes me in the face because that's what he likes to do, that's a crime. If he does it because he hates his life, that's a crime. If he does it because he hates white people, that's a crime. It's not more or less a crime in one case than in the others. In every case, the crime consists of violating my bodily integrity—end of story. So too, if someone steals my mobile phone, that's theft. What difference does it make to me what the motivation of the thief was? What's relevant is that my mobile phone has been stolen. Or suppose that one man assaults a woman and another man assaults another woman and that the physical damage, duration of assault and so on in both cases are as nearly identical as makes no difference. But in one case, the assault is motivated by the assailant's desire to appropriate the woman's purse while in the other case, it's motivated by the assailant's misogynistic belief that women are inherently inferior beings. To punish the second assailant more severely than the first is to punish him for his misogyny which, however much we might disapprove of it morally, is not in itself a criminal offence—at least, not yet.

Whatever fancy footsteps one dances around the legal issues raised by so-called hate crimes, it should be readily apparent that punishing <crime X + hate> by factor delta more severely than <crime X *simpliciter*> makes the hate in <crime X + hate> punishable by factor delta and, since hate is a psychological emotion or attitude, what the law is punishing by the extra weighting are the thoughts of the criminal. Hate crime is thought crime.

Blasphemy bites back!

Which is worse? To physically attack people, perhaps even to murder them, or to say nasty or rude things about their religion? Gosh, that's a tricky question! Hmmmm—let me think! Most people, I suspect, would probably come down on the greater gravity of murder, though who can be entirely sure in this age of universal moral flux?

Libertarians hold as a principle that *all* systems of thought— religious, philosophical, secular, including Libertarianism itself!— should be open for being laughed at, jeered at, held in contempt, ridiculed or otherwise subject to intellectual attack. It doesn't follow from this principle that it is polite or expedient or morally justified to laugh at, jeer at, or hold in contempt or ridicule such systems, and neither does it follow—and I cannot stress this sufficiently— that where such systems are held to be unworthy of credence that it justifies physical attacks on those who adhere to such systems. So, for example, one might consider Catholicism to be hyperbolical nonsense and its adherents stupid and deluded and one may publish one's views trenchantly if one is so minded in print or on the radio or on TV or at meetings of the local Anti-Catholic League. Catholics are unlikely to be particularly appreciative of the expression of such views but tolerating them is the price they pay for living in a free society. Where I just wrote 'Catholicism' one should be able to substitute 'Anglicanism', or 'Methodism' or 'Marxism' or 'Cultural Relativism' or 'Secularism' or 'Climate Changeism' and also, unless one wishes to make invidious and unjustifiable exceptions, 'Islam'.

When some atrocity takes place where the perpetrators of that atrocity are Muslims, such as the *Charlie Hebdo* affair (January 2015), in less than a nano-second, someone is going to tell us that whatever we say, we must be careful not to give expression to what is termed 'Islamophobia.' Writing in 2017, Brendan O'Neill says of the typical response to acts of Islamist terror,

> 'Watch out for an Islamophobic backlash', aloof observers say, their minds always more agitated by the thought of stupid white people saying something rude about Islam than by acts of Islamist mass

murder. 'Don't say anything bad about this wonderful religion or its adherents', they tell us ... [But] ... one of the major problems we face today is not that our society is too mean about Islam, but that it flatters Islam too much ... Islam now enjoys the same kind of moral protection from blasphemy and ridicule that Christianity once (wrongly) enjoyed. (O'Neill 2017)

Free speech may be under threat in Western countries but in some other countries it hardly exists at all. As the London-based Muslim cleric Anjem Choudary wrote in a letter that was published in *USA Today* (January 2015) and copied elsewhere, 'Contrary to popular misconception, Islam does not mean peace but rather means submission to the commands of Allah alone. Therefore, Muslims do not believe in the concept of freedom of expression, as their speech and actions are determined by divine revelation and not based on people's desires.' (Choudary 2015) Mr Choudary is to be congratulated for putting the matter so plainly that even useful-idiot-Islamophiles can hardly miss the point. He then adds, in words that should send a chill up the spine of anyone who hasn't had that anatomical feature surgically removed, 'In an increasingly unstable and insecure world, the potential consequences of insulting the Messenger Muhammad are known to Muslims and non-Muslims alike.' As the staff of *Charlie Hebdo* discovered, the consequences were very far from being merely potential. Lest we be confused as to where the responsibility for the *Charlie Hebdo* massacre resides, Mr Choudary leaves us in no doubt. 'Why,' he asks, 'did the French government allow the magazine *Charlie Hebdo* to continue to provoke Muslims, thereby placing the sanctity of its citizens at risk?' I see. The *Charlie Hebdo* murders were somehow the responsibility of the French Government! The sheer brass-neckery of that question takes my breath away, thankfully, only metaphorically.

We are sometimes told by peace advocates that violence never works. Unfortunately, manifestly pious as that sentiment is, it is also manifestly false. The *Charlie Hebdo* journalists had some pens in their hands which were plainly not mightier than the swords, or rather the Kalashnikovs, of the brothers Kourachi. And the *Jyllands-Posten*, which published the notorious "Danish Cartoons" in 2005 turned down the suggestion that they might reprint the images for, as they remarked blandly, 'violence works'. It is unacceptable in any society that purports to be liberal for the holders of any beliefs, however sacred they may hold their beliefs to be, to be allowed to think that they are licensed to give violent expression to their outrage when their beliefs come under attack.

Attacking a system of thought, religious or otherwise, should not be a criminal offence; attacking the *adherents* of a system of thought should be (and is) criminal. The term *attacking* is used in two quite different ways in the previous sentence. To speak of attacking a system of thought is to describe what is in reality criticism or vulgar abuse in metaphorical terms. To speak of attacking an adherent of a system of thought is to describe a literal, physical assault. The two forms of attack are very different as anyone who has experience both kinds of attack will testify. At the root of hate speech law is the tendency to portray language as a form of violence that sits on a continuum with real physical violence. But verbal abuse and physical abuse are two different kinds of things. The old chant we learnt as children, 'Sticks and stones may break my bones but names will never hurt me' was wrong in one respect and right in another. Name-calling can and does hurt but it hurts in a very different way from the way in which receiving the contents of the magazine of an AK47 full in the chest hurts.

To be clear, the issue is not whether it is impolite or unhelpful or insulting or hurtful to feelings to say nasty or rude things about another's religion or his religious beliefs but whether it should be a matter of law rather than of politeness and civility to prevent people from speaking as they wish on these matters. I am a religious believer myself and I don't enjoy seeing my religious beliefs mocked or derided but I am not prepared to resort to the coercive power of the law to make sure I'm not offended.

You may think that laws on blasphemy among the nations of Europe are either non-existent or are dead letters. Think again. In Ireland, section 36 of the Defamation Act 2009 criminalises the publication or utterance of blasphemous matter. In Austria, section 188 of the Criminal Code called 'Vilification of Religious Teachings', criminalises 'Anyone who publicly disparages a person or thing that is the object of worship of a domestic church or religious society.' Similar legal sentiments can be found in sections 141-142 of the Cypriot Criminal Code, section 10 of the Criminal Code of Finland, article 198 of the Greek Penal Code, article 196 of the Polish Penal Code and article 525 of the Spanish Penal Code. Section 166 of the German criminal code still contains a blasphemy law which shields special religious as well as other philosophical views from criticism or defamation. It reads, '(1) Whosoever publicly or through dissemination of written materials (section 11(3)) defames the religion or ideology of others in a manner that is capable of disturbing the public peace, shall be liable to imprisonment not exceeding three years or a fine. (2) Whosoever publicly or through dissemination of written materials (section 11(3)) defames a church or other religious or ideological association within Germany, or their institutions or customs in a manner that is capable of disturbing the public peace, shall incur the same penalty.'

Are any of these laws still relevant? Yes, decidedly so, a point made with commendable if distressing clarity by a case heard in 2018 by the European Court of Human Rights (ECHR). In October of that year, the ECHR rejected an appeal by a woman (known as E. S. or Mrs S.) who had been convicted in her home country, Austria, of the crime of publicly disparaging religious doctrines. She claimed that her right to freedom of expression under article 10 of the European Convention on Human Rights has been violated by the conviction. Mrs S. had made comments during the course of a seminar offering information on Islam in which she remarked unfavourably on Muhammad's marriage to Aisha. The Regional Criminal Court of Vienna found that she had deliberately sought to degrade Muhammad by disseminating the falsehood that in consummating his marriage with Aisha he was a paedophile. The Court accepted that criticism of child marriages was justifiable, but it also held Mrs S. had wrongly 'accused *a subject of religious worship* of having a primary sexual interest in children's bodies.' Her comments about Muhammad not only constituted 'a malicious violation of the spirit of tolerance,' but were also a threat to religious peace in Austria. (Emphasis added)

Muhammad a subject of religious worship! That statement betrays an astonishing ignorance of Islam's robust rejection of shirk, the deification or worship of anyone or anything besides the singular Allah. A Muslim, Qanta Ahmed remarked that 'The ECHR also claims that "the applicant had suggested that Muhammad was not a worthy subject of worship." Well, that's absolutely fine by me. After all, Muslims don't worship the Prophet: the Quran is clear that God is the sole entity of worship.' (Ahmed 2018)

Here, surely, was an opportunity for the ECHR to give the obnoxious Austrian law the order of the boot. But no! The 7-judge ECHR rejected Mrs S.'s application and, moreover, did so unanimously! (see European Court of Human Rights, October 2018) The Court made the usual nauseatingly pious observations regarding freedom of expression but went on to say that the exercise of that freedom carried with it duties and responsibilities, including, it seems, 'the duty to avoid as far as possible an expression that is, in regard to objects of veneration, gratuitously offensive to others and profane.' The ECHR also stated that where criticism of religion takes the form of what it termed 'an improper or even abusive attack on an object of religious veneration' it should be considered as exceeding the bounds of acceptable expression, since it is 'likely to incite religious intolerance.'

Was Mrs S.'s remark that Muhammad liked to have sex with children an abusive attack? Yes, said the Court, noting that this remark was without factual basis, a comment which is somewhat surprising given that there is a tradition (a contested tradition to be sure) that Muhammad's marriage with Aisha was consummated when the girl was just nine years old. While rejecting the accusation of paedophilia directed against Muhammad, Qanta Ahmed notes, 'The ECHR would presumably be surprised to learn that far worse criticism is levelled at Aisha by some Shia Muslims, for whom she remains a polarising figure.' (Ahmed 2018)

The Court also argued that Mrs S.'s remark also went well 'beyond the permissible limits of an objective debate' and amounted to 'an abusive attack on the Prophet of Islam, which ... ' and here the ECHR agreed with the Austrian court, 'was capable of stirring up prejudice and putting at risk religious peace.' Thus they concluded, E.S.'s conviction was not a violation of article 10 of the European Convention on Human Rights.

Simon Cottee's critical assessment of the ECHR's judgement in *The Atlantic* (October 2018) is commendably restrained but substantially accurate. His conclusion is that ' ... the ECHR's judgment is not wholly convincing ... ', a conclusion which, in my opinion, is the epitome of British understatement! Consider, for example, Cottee says, the court's complaint that

> E.S.'s [Mrs S's] statements [about Muhammad] 'were not phrased in a neutral manner aimed at being an objective contribution to a public debate concerning child marriages.' This is clearly true, but it's hard to see how this is remotely relevant to the case or why the ECHR should lament the absence of objectivity in a seminar on Islam sponsored by a right-wing party in Austria. Who cares if E.S. said things that didn't meet the standards of an 'objective contribution to a public debate'? Clearly there is a whole range of expression that falls dismally below such standards, and yet we should still want to protect the right of individuals to engage in it. Thus the notion of certain kinds of expression, in the ECHR's words, 'going beyond the permissible limits of an objective debate' seems tendentiously and worryingly narrow.

Exactly so. Narrow indeed, and seemingly tailored to the specifics of the case. But I would go much further. The ECHR, in its craven and none-too-subtle bowing to what is, in effect, Islamist pressure, has embedded the principle of 'freedom of speech *but...*' in European Human Rights law. It was undoubtedly correct in coming to the conclusion that Mrs S had been properly found guilty under Austrian law but it was shame-inducingly incorrect in its implicit acceptance that this law was not, as it manifestly is, a violation of the right to free expression embodied in a. 10 of the European Convention on Human Rights.

Commenting on this remarkable judgement, Qanta Ahmed remarked that 'the ECHR's agreement with an Austrian court that offensive comments about the Prophet Mohammed were "beyond the permissible limits of an objective debate" has handed a big victory to both Islamists and Islamophobes—while infantilising believing Muslims everywhere.' She continued, 'This ruling could have wide-ranging—and unforeseen—implications, delivering a victory for those who do wish to criminalise criticism of Islam.' She concluded, 'Ultimately, the ECHR's logic rests on a depressing assumption that Europe's Muslims are somehow incapable of intellectual debate and too fragile to hear criticisms of their religion. Yet this scrutiny is crucial for exposing Islamism—the totalitarian imposter of Islam—and countering its evils.'

Blasphemy in the UK

If you want to visit the UK, then don't insult Allah, whatever you do. Lauren Southern did precisely that in March 2018 when she gave out a leaflet in Luton making rude remarks about Allah, for which crime she was banned from Britain because, it was claimed, her behaviour posed a threat 'to the fundamental interests of society'. What would those fundamental interests be, one wonders? What is so special about Allah? It appears that Southern was questioned under Schedule 7 of the Terrorism Act though it is somewhat difficult to see just what it was about her planned activities that might have constituted terrorism. The section of the Act under which she was held allows detention and questioning for up to nine hours. Brendan O'Neill remarks, 'That such a repressive measure was allegedly deployed in the questioning of someone for distributing *leaflets*, for speech, should horrify anyone who cares about liberty. This effectively treats speech as terror, ideas as violence, mere words as things to be kept out of the nation, setting a terrible precedent for free speech in this country.'! (O'Neill 2018)

On 23 February 2019, Oluwole Ilesanmi, a Christian street preacher, was arrested for perpetrating a breach of the peace. How did that happen? Well, in the course of his preaching, he made some references to Islam which appeared to anger a passer-by who then accosted him. A woman who filmed the incident said that she was afraid that Ilesanmi was about to be attacked. The police arrived and arrested, not the aggressive passer-by but Ilesanmi! (see Twitter February 2019) Whatever one thinks of street preachers—and most people just regard them as an urban nuisance and just ignore them— one might have though that it was Mr Ilesanmi and not the enraged passer-by who was the victim of aggression. Of particular interest were the comments of the arresting officers. When Mr Ilesanmi pointed out that he was just preaching the truth, one officer said that nobody wanted to listen to that. When Mr Ilesanmi objected to his Bible being taken from him, he was told, 'You should have thought about that before being racist.' After his arrest, Mr Ilesanmi was driven to a place on the outskirts of London and then released or, in police-speak, 'de-arrested'!

So, why *was* Mr Ilesanmi arrested. According to Tom Goodenough, Acting Superintendent Neil Billany said, 'The Met respects and upholds the rights of all individuals to practise freedom of speech and this includes street preachers of all religions and backgrounds.' Well, that's good to hear. But, and there is always a *but*, 'if the language someone uses is perceived as being a potential hate crime, it is only right that we investigate.' (Goodenough 2019) A *potential* hate crime? Really? On his own admission, Mr Ilesanmi called Islam an 'aberration' and referred to Allah as an 'idol', not pleasant hearing, to be sure, if you are a Muslim but then, unless you were imprisoned in a nearby stocks or had your feet glued to the pavement, you couldn't be forced to listen to any of what Mr Ilesanmi had to say. In a similar incident in 2017, two Christian street preachers criticised Islam while preaching in Bristol and were convicted of a religiously aggravated public order offence. Their conviction was subsequently overturned by a judge who said he was 'conscious of the right of freedom of speech and freedom of expression'.

Whatever one makes of what these people said or intended to say, there can be no doubt that they will be inhibited in future from saying it. If you were to take the view that what they are saying is so obviously lunatical and obnoxious that there can be no harm in preventing them from saying it on UK soil, then it might be a good idea to think again. Today it is those idiots, those freaks, those religious nuts (as a good liberal might think of them) who are subject to legal intimidation, but tomorrow it could be that very same liberal and his gang of idiots and freaks. If we allow the government or its minions to determine what may or may not be said, then there is no guarantee that it is only the crackpots you disapprove of who'll be on the receiving end of the heavy hand of the state.

As Brendan O'Neill has noted, blasphemy laws were originally intended to protect Christianity from insult and attack. Those days have long gone. You can say pretty much whatever you want about Christianity in the confident expectation of not having the police knock on your door. But you are far more likely to get a visit from the local constabulary if you were, on the basis of your reading of the Christian scriptures, to publicly condemn homosexuality as sinful.

Freedom of speech but...

When I was a boy, you could buy a very large, round piece of candy that you stuck in your mouth. It lasted seemingly for ever and while it was in your mouth, it prevented coherent speech. For that reason it was known colloquially, if inelegantly, as a gob-stopper! The liberal left has the linguistic equivalent of the gob-stopper. Christopher Akehurst puts it well when he writes,

> 'Racist', 'sexist' and 'phobic', the last one with various prefixes, are the lexical building blocks of leftist discourse. Three little words and their variants, but eliminate them from the vocabulary and the Left would have nothing much to say. It would have only its riots and assaults to make its voice heard and express what passes for its opinions. But since those words do exist, they are played for all they are worth as a means of shouting down non-leftists. This means that social problems that the Left refuses to recognise as such, usually because they suit its purposes, go undebated, because to discuss them is invariably labelled 'racist', 'sexist' or 'something-phobic'. (Akehurst 2018)

To be accused of any of these dastardly crimes is a classic strategy used to deflect attention from the substantive issues, by which rhetorical device rational discussion can be strangled at source.

Who does not love freedom of speech or rather who, apart from Muslims à la Anjem Choudary, does not love it? The answer is, all those who are freedom of speech 'but-heads'. 'Freedom of speech, yes,' they say, '*but....*' and then come all the exceptions. Tanya Cohen, to whom I referred earlier, is a fine example of a freedom of speech but-head unless, as seems unlikely, her screed is intended to be deeply satirical. She writes, 'Like any sensible person, I am a strong believer in the unalienable right to freedom of speech and I understand that defending freedom of speech is the most important when it's speech that many people do not want to hear (like, for example, pro-LGBT speech in Russia). Freedom of speech is the core of any democratic society, and it's important that freedom of speech be strongly respected and upheld. Censorship in all of its forms is something that must always be fiercely opposed.'

So far so good (apart from the tendentious LGBT example, but let that pass). Now comes the *but*; 'But we must never confuse hate speech with freedom of speech. Speech that offends, insults, demeans, threatens, disrespects, incites hatred or violence, and/or violates basic human rights and freedoms has absolutely no place in even the freest society. In fact, it has no place in any free society, as bigotry is fundamentally anti-freedom by its very nature. The human right to freedom of speech must always be balanced against the human rights to dignity, respect, honor, non-discrimination, and freedom from hatred.' (Cohen 2015)

In this remarkable passage, freedom of speech suffers the death of a thousand buts. As a writer in *The New Criterion* puts it, '"I am for free speech, but not 'hate speech'/speech that offends Mohammed/ speech that insults Greens/speech that mocks, satirizes, ridicules, and laughs at some PC icon," etc. Then you are not for free speech at all, and your "but" is merely a species of capitulation pretending to redemptive conceptual nuance. Free speech is by nature offensive speech, at least potentially. If it couldn't offend, if it couldn't insult, it also couldn't enlighten.' (Anon. 2015)

Mandatory speech

Not being permitted to say certain things is one thing, and a very bad thing at that; being compelled under legal penalty to say certain things is quite another, and a much worse, thing. Hate speech laws are primarily laws that *prohibit* certain types of expression but more intrusive are those laws that *compel* certain forms of speech so that failing to speak in a certain way attracts censure and legal sanctions.

The New York City Commission on Human Rights has issued a comprehensive diktat on this matter. The Commission tells us that New York City's Human Rights Law (NYCHRL) prohibits 'unlawful discrimination in public accommodations, housing and employment on the basis of gender. Gender is defined as one's 'actual or perceived sex and shall also include a person's gender identity, self-image, appearance, behavior or expression, whether or not that gender identity, self-image, appearance, behavior or expression is different from that traditionally associated with the legal sex assigned to that person at birth.'

Under the NYCHRL, the Commission requires employers and entities covered by the legislation to use people's preferred names, pronouns and titles regardless of people's sex that was assigned (their word!) at birth, their anatomy, their gender, their medical history, their appearance, or the sex indicated on their forms of identification. The Commission notes that most individuals and many transgender people use female or male pronouns and titles but that some transgender and gender non-conforming people prefer to use pronouns other than he/him/his or she/her/hers. According to the Commission, there are a number of ways in which you can go wrong, only one of which is of interest to our discussion here and that is the 'Intentional or repeated refusal to use an individual's preferred name, pronoun or title. For example, repeatedly calling a transgender woman "him" or "Mr." after she has made clear which pronouns and title she uses.'

Names are not really a problem. An individual may use any name he, she or it wishes and, barring certain specific circumstances, such as extreme vulgarity (calling yourself, say 'F@$% Me!' and requiring people to address you by that name), some titles such as 'Dr' or 'Your Highness' where the person isn't a doctor or royalty, or having names consisting of 42 syllables ('Call me "supercalifragilisticexpialid-ocioussupercalifragilisticexpialidocioussupercalifragilisticexpialido-cious"'), it's little more than a matter of elementary politeness to use a person's preferred name. Pronouns, however, are a different matter.

What limits, if any, are there to what pronouns, old or new, may be required by the NYCHRL? No principled ones, it seems for a person may prefer whatever pronouns he/she/it/ze/zir/they wish. In some places, personal pronominal police-actions have now reached a level of insanity that makes satire almost impossible. Failure to use so-called 'gender-neutral' pronouns, such as *xu, hir, ze, nir, hiser* and so on, by which a given person desires to be addressed, can be (and has been) deemed a form of discrimination and a breach of human rights. Of course, a moment's thought will reveal the absurdity of the policy of demanding, on pain of sanctions, that person X be addressed by a chosen pronoun, Y. Apart from the practical problem of requir-ing innocent third parties to remember a possibly impossibly large number of possible pronouns, thus defeating one of the purposes for which pronouns came into being in the first place, what is to prevent a pronoun warrior from demanding to be addressed as *gutface, glinky* or *gloopiness the 3rd*? Taken to its extreme, such Humpty-Dumptyish linguistic voluntarism will inevitably lead to the decline of person-al pronouns altogether and saddle those of us who wish to avoid persecution with the unenviable task of endlessly repeating name after name after name.

Failure to observe the Commission's requirements can result in stiff penalties; up to $125,000 for basic violations but as much as

$250,000 if your violation is wilful, wanton or malicious! What all this nonsense comes down to is that one can be legally forced to say what one does not want to say, to subscribe to an ideology one does not want to subscribe to, or to endorse a political message that one does not believe in. If you are not prepared to do this you risk incurring severe financial penalties.

In the United Kingdom, Martin Evans, the *Telegraph*'s crime correspondent, reported in March 2019 that Caroline Farrow, whom Evans describes as 'a devout Catholic and mother of five' has been asked to attend a police interview after being accused of 'using the wrong pronoun to describe a transgender girl' and thus misgendering her. (One wonders, by the way, why it's worth reporting that Mrs Farrow is a 'devout Catholic' unless it is to suggest perhaps that saying a man is a man and a woman is a woman is some bizarre and idiosyncratic or outmoded religious belief instead of a plain and simple matter of biology! But let that pass.) Mrs Farrow was advised by officials of the Surrey police force that they were investigating an allegation that she had made transphobic comments on Twitter. Under the terms of the *Malicious Communication Act*, she may have committed a possible hate crime and could face a two-year prison sentence.

This palpable nonsense is to be reprobated as a waste of police time, a point made by Sara Thornton who left her post as head of the UK's National Police Chief's Council in 2019 and also by the Metropolitan Police Commissioner, Cressida Dick. But even if the police had world enough and time, such matters are not the proper object of criminal investigations. In an editorial, the *Telegraph* (20 March 2019) commented that while Mrs Farrow's alleged 'misgendering' might be a matter of concern to the two individuals involved, it was difficult to see by what possible measure of sanity it became a matter for a police investigation. The editorial writer went on to say that it wasn't the job of the police to dance to the tune of the minuscule but militant trans lobby but to uphold the law of the land. The editorial writer also noted that hate-crime laws 'were introduced to protect minority groups from abuse but are being used to shut down perfectly legitimate opinion, for instance on the rights and wrongs of gay marriage, as in the "gay cake" case in Northern Ireland.' And to this case and its American companion we now turn.

Masterpiece Cakeshop and Asher's Bakery

The issue of compelled speech came to a head in some cases concerning, of all things, cakes! In 2012 in the USA, two men asked Jack Phillips and his Masterpiece Cakeshop to design a custom wedding cake for their marriage to each other. Mr Phillips, who believes marriage is the lifelong union of one man and one woman, declined for reasons of conscience to design the cake, though he was perfectly willing to supply anything already in his shop or, indeed, to create a custom cake for another occasion if the couple so desired. The Colorado Civil Rights Commission took a dim view of Mr Phillips's refusal and instructed him to design wedding cakes that celebrate same-sex marriage and to do various forms of administrative penance for his wrongdoing. (It is interesting to note that the Commission was of the view that cake designers could lawfully refuse to design cakes with anti-same-sex marriage messages on them!) This case is just one of many in which attempts have been made to force various businesses—guest house owners, printers, florists—to cooperate with activities of which they conscientiously disapprove.

The Phillips case eventually reached the US Supreme Court which, in June 2018, found in favour of Mr Phillips. The decision was restricted to the specific circumstances of the case and so we must wait to see if the Court will support the broader position of businesses that refuse to supply specific services for specific purposes to specific people. The justices held (7 to 2) that the Commission had violated Mr Phillips's First Amendment rights. The dissenters were—I know this will come as a surprise to you—Justices Ginsberg and Sotomayor. In his majority opinion, Justice Kennedy said that the broader issues would have to await further elaboration in the courts. In a similar case, Barronelle Stutzman, a florist in Richland, Washington, appealed a State Supreme Court ruling that found she violated state law in refusing to provide wedding flowers for two men who were about to be married. The United States Supreme Court vacated a Washington State ruling against her and sent the case back to the Washington Supreme Court for reconsideration in the context of their Masterpiece Cakeshop decision.

In the UK, the case corresponding to the Masterpiece Cakeshop was that of Asher's Bakery in Belfast. It was settled unanimously by the UK's Supreme Court in October 2018. (see Supreme Court,

10 October 2018) The bakery had refused to make a wedding cake for a homosexual couple that contained the slogan, 'Support Gay Marriage'. An action had been taken against Asher's Bakery by Gareth Lee and it had succeeded at the level of the county court and the Northern Ireland Court of Appeal. However, Lady Hale, delivering the judgement of the UK's Supreme Court said that 'The bakery could not refuse to provide a cake—or any other of their products—to Mr Lee because he was a gay man or because he supported gay marriage. But that important fact does not amount to a justification for something completely different—obliging them to supply a cake iced with a message with which they profoundly disagreed.' (§55 of the judgement) Earlier in the judgement, Lady Hale had noted that

> The objection was not to Mr Lee because he, or anyone with whom he associated, held a political opinion supporting gay marriage. The objection was to being required to promote the message on the cake. The less favourable treatment was afforded to the message not to the man .... The situation is not comparable to people being refused jobs, accommodation or business simply because of their religious faith. It is more akin to a Christian printing business being required to print leaflets promoting an atheist message. (§47 of the judgement)

Towards the end of the judgement, Lady Hale adverted to the US Masterpiece Cakeshop case and characterised it in in these words.

> The important message from the Masterpiece Bakery case is that there is a clear distinction between refusing to produce a cake conveying a particular message, for any customer who wants such a cake, and refusing to produce a cake for the particular customer who wants it because of that customer's characteristics .... If and to the extent that there was discrimination on grounds of political opinion, no justification has been shown for the compelled speech which would be entailed for imposing civil liability for refusing to fulfil the order. (§62 of the judgement)

Interesting as these cases are, the courts are limited in the decisions they can reach because they accept that legislatures can make laws that mandate compulsory association. From a libertarian perspective, the issue here is not in the first instance freedom of speech or freedom of conscience or anything of that nature. It's simply a matter of property rights. From a libertarian perspective, you can do as you will with your property, provided that in so doing, you don't violate the ZAP. We don't expect to be dictated to when it comes to our choice of friends or sexual partners. We don't expect to be told what music to listen to and have that recommendation enforced by law. From a libertarian point of view, you can buy from and sell to whomever you please provided the other party agrees to the transaction. You can associate with whomever you please *and you can refuse to associate with whomever you please.* Of course, you must accept the non-aggressive consequences of your decisions. If other people disapprove of your decisions, expect them to voice their disapproval and, if need be, to act upon it. If your decision is to refuse a person service for reason X, then you must expect those who espouse X to express their dissatisfaction with your decision and, provided their dissatisfaction is expressed non-aggressively, you are going to have to tolerate it.

Wouldn't this permit prejudice? Yes. But there are ways of dealing with prejudice other than by legal means. Business is business, and I don't have to like particular persons to sell them a pair of shoes or even a cake. Irrational prejudices will have to be paid for in loss of custom, loss of friendships, loss of social amenities and, in the extreme, boycotting and isolation. In the early Middle Ages, the Venetians traded with the Muslim countries of Egypt and the Levant—religious differences were not allowed to get in the way of trade.

No one should be coerced into any form of relationship with another, whether that relationship is personal or political or social or business. No law should force you to be friends with X or to be enemies with Y or to join a particular political party or to do business with those you would prefer not to do business with, whatever the reasons for your choices. These reasons may be commendable or not. That's another matter.

As things stand, if you are in business, the state forces you to do business with others whether you would prefer to do business with them or not. It's hardly surprising that the state takes this stand since it itself is essentially an institution based on coercion. Those who advocate legal coercion would do well to remember that if they are willing to override someone's choices because they or their agents determine that the basis on which those choices are made are discriminatory or prejudiced, they have no principled ground to stand on if others, when they get their hands on the levers of power, override *their* choices.

Free Speech in the University

War is peace!
Freedom is slavery!
Ignorance is strength!
—*George Orwell*

Our free-thinking students?

According to the *Oxford English Dictionary, free speech* simply means having the freedom to express one's opinions without censorship or legal penalty. What could be controversial about that? Surely this comes into the category of motherhood and apple pie—everyone's in favour of it. Well, perhaps, perhaps not. It depends upon the choices one makes when conflicts arise and free speech is only one good among others. Everyone is in favour of free speech *except*..... and then, as we've seen, free speech can die the death of a thousand buts.

In a survey conducted by the online magazine *Spiked*, over half of the UK's 115 universities were considered to actively censor speech and ideas. The situation is not dissimilar in the USA. In a 2018 poll of college students sponsored by the American Council on Education, majorities of students when asked said they supported *both* free speech and inclusion & diversity, but when asked which is more important, 53 percent said inclusion & diversity and only 46 percent said free speech! (More on inclusion & diversity below.) This is a striking finding. College students used to be gung ho on free speech. Now, college campuses have been transformed from being those places most in favour of free speech to being among those places least in favour of it. Not only are there restrictive speech codes operating under the oversight of college bureaucracies, ostensibly to prevent offensive speech, but students have taken it upon themselves to police each other's speech. Another significant change from the past is that free speech used to receive support from groups that perceived themselves as being disadvantaged, groups largely on the left of the political spectrum. Now, for these students, supporting free speech is tantamount to supporting racists or sexists or perpetrators of hate speech or other kinds of evil-speaking people so that the defence of free speech and its vindication has come to be perceived as primarily a right-wing or conservative or libertarian concern.

It may come as a surprise to you or even a shock—but then again, it may not—to find that most students in American colleges would support banning speakers who use hate speech. Even more startling is the finding that a third of students support the use of violence to prevent such speech! But as the Foundation for Individual Rights in Education (FIRE) points out, 'There is no consensus as to what qualifies as "hate speech," leading to vaguely-worded speech codes that can be applied to virtually all forms of political expression protected under First Amendment standards.'

It's not only in the USA that students have ambivalent or largely negative attitudes towards free speech. In November 2017, the *Telegraph* reported that students at Magdalen College, Oxford, had voted to introduce compulsory workshops for incoming students. Ah, you will perhaps think, no doubt the topics of these workshops will be remedial grammar and spelling and some history and geography and a little basic logic and how to assess informal arguments, and they will emphasise the absolute necessity of keeping one's mind open before it is firmly closed. If that's what you thought, prepare to be disappointed! These mandatory workshops will instruct new students on the temptations presented by the new deadly sins of racism, cultural appropriation and implicit bias. The bland assumption underlying this bizarre and insufferably paternalistic exercise is that, unless rescued from the slough of moral darkness by their elders and betters—older students, in case you didn't recognise the description—incoming students will be racist, their actions governed by bias (implicit and explicit) and, unless forcibly restrained, they will be liable to appropriate the culture of others—a most peculiar form of theft. (More on student aberrations and on cultural appropriation below.)

The difference between males and females on the issue of free speech is also striking, with 61% of men being generally in favour of free speech compared to only 35% of women. This is all the more significant in that women now make up a majority of students, as well as comprising the majority of those university administrators who are charged with enforcing their university's speech and sexual assault codes. Why the difference between men and women on this issue? Perhaps women are socialised to be more agreeable, more consensus-seeking than men? Perhaps men, now perceiving themselves as possible victims of behaviour control by means of speech codes favour free speech as a possible tool of self-defence? Who can tell? It is often assumed that a world with greater opportunities for women would be a friendlier and freer world though the evidence to support this claim is somewhat fugitive. Friendlier? Perhaps—as long as you think and act in the prescribed manner. Freer? Well, if the polls are anything to go by, I wouldn't be too sure about that.

In prehistoric times, before we decided that wisdom was an attribute of youth, we used to think that on many if not most matters, people should be free to make up their own minds. Points of view could be expressed, arguments presented, evidence assessed, and minds finally made up. True, not everyone wished to engage in this process but those who wanted to be regarded as educated recognised that one of education's aims was to fit them to take part in the discussions and arguments that are a constitutive part of the workings of a free society. But thanks to the wisdom of our youth, we now know better. This 'free speech is good' nonsense was merely a way of disguising the repressive power that was exercised by the powerful and the privileged over the powerless and the oppressed. Free speech, which has been regarded as a staple element in our liberal polities for donkey's years, turns out to be simply a stalking donkey for the machinations of the far right!

Many young people seem to think that the repression of freedom of speech is no big deal; that is, of course, provided that *their* freedom of speech is not under threat and that they and their enlightened brethren are the ones doing the repressing! Once the principle of censorship is accepted, however, the only matter to settle is who or what is to be censored and who is to do the censoring. Today you may be the censor and your unspeakable enemies the censored; but what's to prevent the roles being reversed tomorrow? In addition, the young won't be young forever nor is it likely once they confront the responsibilities of adulthood, that their views will remain as infantile as they now are. What then will protect the speech of the now sober, tax-paying and mortgage-bound middle-aged ex-young? Just as the village layabout said he loved work so much he could watch people working all day, so too, repression of free speech isn't a problem—as long as you are the one doing the repressing. Today's adherents to the new censorious orthodoxy seem to assume that they'll always be young and always right-thinking (that is 'right' as opposed to 'wrong' and not to 'left') and always pure and uncontaminated. Why should they worry about censorship when they're always going to be the ones doing the censoring?

Desperate to avoid hurting other people's feelings

In the *Guardian*, Gaby Hinsliff remarks, 'Going back to speak to students at my old university last year, I was struck less by a zealous desire to police speech than by their desperation to avoid hurting other people's feelings by displaying even inadvertent prejudice. They came across not as hysterical snowflakes, but as earnest and thoughtful.' (Hinsliff 2017) Seriously, Ms Hinsliff! You don't think that there's something just a little bit, well, pathological about a desperate desire to avoid hurting other people's feelings—not just normal well-mannered efforts to do so but a *desperate* desire? To see how desperate students can be to avoid saying anything that might hurt someone's feelings, here is a partial transcript of interviews conducted by a 5' 9" white man from the Family Policy Institute of Washington on the campus of the University of Washington. As you will see, the interviewer's sex, height and ethnicity are relevant to the questions asked and the answers given. (see Family Policy Institute 2016)

Dramatis personae: **I**: interviewer; **H**: a young woman; **B**: a young man; **P**: a young man; **C**: a young woman; **T**: a young man: **G**: a young woman: **Z**: a young woman, and **W**: a young man. The interview begins:

I: *If I told you I was a woman, what would your response be?*
H: Good for you! Ok, like, yeah!
B: Nice to meet you!
P: Probably like, what? Really?

C: I don't have a problem with it.
T: I'd ask you how you came to that conclusion.

I: *If I told you I was Chinese, what would your response be?*
H: I mean I might be a little surprised but I'd say, like—good for you, yeah, be who you are.
G: I would maybe think you had some Chinese ancestor.
T: I would ask you how you [indistinct] came to that conclusion and *why* you came to that conclusion.
Z: I would have a lot of questions. Just because on the outside I would assume that you're a white man.

I: *If I told you I was seven years old, what would your response be?*
H: [Surprised face—initially, no verbal response, then, later] If you feel seven at heart, then so be it, good for you.
G: Umm, I wouldn't believe that immediately.
W: Uhh, I probably wouldn't believe it but, I mean, I... it wouldn't really bother me to go out of my way and tell you, 'No, you're wrong', I just feel like, 'OK, he wants to be seven years old.'

I: *If I told you I'm 6' 5" (he's actually 5' 9"), what would you say?*
C: [taken aback. No verbal response]
Z: *That* I would question.
I: *Why?*
Z: [laughing] Because you're not! No, I don't think you are 6' 5".
G: If you truly believe you're 6' 5", I don't believe it's harmful; I think it's fine if you believe that. It doesn't matter to me if you think you're taller than you are.

I: *So, you'd be willing to tell me I'm wrong?*
G: I wouldn't tell you you're wrong.
C: No, but I'd say that I don't think that you are.
H: I feel like that's not my place as, like another human, to say that someone is wrong or to draw lines or boundaries.
W: No, I mean I wouldn't just go like, 'Oh, you're wrong' [indistinct] or it's wrong to believe in it because, again, it doesn't really bother me what you want to think about your height or anything.

I: *So, I can be a Chinese woman...*
Z: [laughing] Sure...
I: *But I can't be a 6' 5" Chinese woman?*

P: ...Yes.

T: If you thoroughly debated me or explained why you felt that you are 6' 5" I feel like I'd be very open to saying that you are 6' 5", or Chinese, or a woman!

One doesn't know whether to laugh or weep! These students are obviously pleasant and well-mannered young people who don't want to offend others by telling them that they're wrong but they seem utterly incapable of saying, 'Look, I don't want to hurt your feelings and I'm not planning to assault you physically or shout abuse at you but let's get this straight—you're *not* Chinese, you're *not* a woman and you're *not* 6' 5"'. How difficult would it be to say that? What's the betting that if you asked them about the right-on hot button topics where there is currently a liberal consensus—abortion or date rape—you wouldn't find them anywhere near as reticent to tell you what's what. The editorial writer in *The New Criterion* describes this video as 'hilarious' (which it is) but also as 'terrifying' (which it also is) because 'it reveals the extent to which the insanity of "identity politics" has corrupted judgment and language. The ambition behind this nonsense is magical: that by the proper incantatory spells, reality itself might be altered ... We may well be on the road to Chesterton's men who are "too mentally modest to believe in the multiplication table," but two times two still equals four, a man is a man, not a woman, and a short Caucasian is a short Caucasian, not a tall Asian. One didn't always have to go to college to learn these things. Perhaps the moral is, one still doesn't.' (Anon. 2016)

Campus restrictions on speech

Do universities have the right to ban speakers if they so choose? Of course! To the extent that any institution or business belongs entirely to Tom and Dick and Harriet, then on the basis of the 'My House, My Rules' (MHMR) maxim, Tom, Dick and Harriet have the right to decide who may speak on their premises and use their facilities and who may not and what may be said and what may not. Whether Tom, Dick and Harriet are right to make the decisions that they do is quite another matter! However, if the institution or business is in receipt of funding from another person or body (for example, a government) then, since such funding comes with strings (or hawsers!) attached, it has given contractual hostages to fortune, good or bad, and must abide by the conditions attached to such funding.

Freedom of speech and rational enquiry are constituent aspects of the intellectual life of the university so that if either comes under threat, it is a matter of general concern. A report of the UK's Parliamentary Joint Committee on Human Rights states that intolerant attitudes, unnecessary bureaucracy and regulatory complexity hamper speech on university campuses. Among the factors inhibiting free speech are students unions' policies and official university policies. No news there, then. It should be pointed out that not all that many people have actually been prohibited from speaking on campuses but the whole point of so-called No Platform policies is that they operate to ensure that the wrong kind of people are not invited in the first place! Are concerns about the limitation on free speech on university campuses exaggerated, then? Well, let's see. Over a third of campuses ban legal groups, almost half limit criticism of religion as long as it's not Christianity and the issue of Safe Spaces is large and growing. More on these topics as we proceed.

Let's look at some examples. The University of Michigan has an elaborate investigatory and disciplinary apparatus that exists to prevent or punish speech that some students consider to be demeaning or hurtful. An organisation called Speech First has charged the University with unconstitutional prior restraint, alleging that regulations that prohibit verbal conduct that supposedly victimises or jeopardises a social climate that is safe and inclusive is simply too vague to give any student effective notice of what precisely is prohibited and, perhaps more importantly, what is permitted. Students (and staff) are likely to find out that they've transgressed these regulations only *after* they've done so. The effect of such vague regulations is, of course, to induce people to self-censor any form of verbal expression that might be prohibited and this is hardly conducive to an atmosphere of free speech.

In March 2018, an American-Israeli writer, Yaron Brook and a popular YouTuber, Carl Benjamin were supposed to address the King's College London (KCL) Libertarian Society. This they were unable to do, being prevented by a group of people who claimed that Brook and Benjamin were fascists and white supremacists. This suppression of free speech wasn't achieved by polite means but rather by violent disruption and intimidation. It is one thing to express disagreement peacefully; it is quite another to undertake by violence to prevent points of view other than your own from ever being heard. Of course, such disruptors should be prevented from disrupting and, if they persist in their violent activities, expelled from the universities of which they are purportedly students. What tends to happen, however, is that those who wish to speak freely and those who wish to hear them are the ones who are punished by not being able to do as they wish, while the violent disruptors achieve their aims without any significant deleterious consequences to themselves.

In April 2018, in a wonderful example of incestuous irony, one of King's College London's own lecturers was unable to give a talk on free speech to the Libertarian Society in his own university! Dr Adam Perkins, who is a specialist in the neurobiology of personality, was to have spoken to the Society about the importance of free speech in science. The university postponed the event after carrying out a risk assessment. Dr Perkins was deemed to be a 'high risk' speaker because his writings are considered to be controversial.

A month earlier, protestors stormed another KCL Libertarian Society event that was to have featured the YouTuber Sargon of Akkad (aka Carl Benjamin). The protestors smashed windows and threw smoke bombs, setting off the fire alarms. The event was to have featured a discussion of Ayn Rand's Objectivism between Benjamin and the chairman of the Board of Directors at the Ayn Rand Institute, Dr Brooks. The President of the Libertarian Society, Danny Al-Khafaji, said 'This was an extremely well organised protest. They jumped over the barriers, smashed windows and a door. The security guards on the door were attacked, two were hospitalised … They stormed in, went straight to the stage, up to me and the speakers and started harassing us and the audience. Fire alarms went off—they had dropped smoke bombs.'

When one hears the word 'Marshal', one thinks of Westerns and shootouts outside the saloon or at least I do. But if you do think as I do, think so no longer. For King's College London now has its own set of Marshals, paid for by the KCL Students' Union, to ensure that talks sponsored by student groups don't breach (or in the advertisement's idiosyncratic spelling), 'breech' its Safe Space policies. All student-run events are supposed to be inclusive and supportive. Furthermore, it is mandatory to have balance of opinion at every event. Comical as the idea of Students' Union Marshals seems, and is, it yet appears that these Marshals actually have the power to eject people from meetings, even invited speakers, if they don't comply with the inclusive and supportive and balanced policy! The KCL Libertarian Society commented, with some justice, that the system of Marshal monitoring 'creates an environment in which students are treated as if they need chaperones and supervisors to hold their events, which is deeply patronising and takes away student autonomy.' (Rose) These Marshals must, it seems, be ready to take immediate action if any speaker breaches the safe space policy by expressing prohibited opinions. Such prohibited opinions could include comments that are considered to be derogatory about sexual orientation or gender identity or socio-economic status or disability or age or God only knows what else. It's not clear what immediate action the Marshals are expected to take if someone blasphemes.

Not all students are appreciative of the Students' Union's effort on their behalf. In October 2017, a talk given by the Conservative MP, Jacob Rees-Mogg, was monitored by the Marshals and one student commented, satirically, 'Massive thanks to KCLSU for providing a fantastic safe space yesterday! I know that without the five Safe Space Marshals working tirelessly, I definitely couldn't have listened to Jacob Rees-Mogg without having my feelings seriously hurt!'

In 2018, the City University of New York (CUNY) School of Law Federalist Society invited Josh Blackman to speak on a panel discussion about theories of constitutional interpretation. Mr Blackman planned to speak on the theory of Constitutional interpretation known as Originalism. However, no other professors were willing to participate in the event (what a surprise!) so Mr Blackman suggested an event on free speech on campus. Still no professorial contributors volunteered to participate. It is more than a little ironic that Mr Blackman's talk about free speech on campus was disrupted and heckled so that he was prevented from speaking freely on campus about free speech on campus. The highlight of the evening has to have been the point at which Mr Blackman said, 'you can support something as a matter of policy ... but find that the law does not permit it. And then the answer is to change the law.' At which a student shouted, 'F*** the law.' Mr Blackman was, naturally, somewhat taken aback at the sentiment expressed thus rudely and crudely. 'F*** the law?' he said. 'That's a very odd thing. You are all in law school. And it is a bizarre thing to say f*** the law when you are in law school.' One student then said, 'I don't support this guy' but 'I want to ask him a very hard question. And we should all try to ask him very hard questions. Like about the notion of legal objectivity.' The protesters then heckled and shouted over *this* student! Eventually, like children exhausted from their tantrums, they finally left and Mr Blackman then took questions from students for over an hour, addressing such issues as originalism, texualism, affirmative action, criminal procedure, the separation of powers and other topics that one would think might have been of interest to some of those who protested and from which they might have learned something about the discipline of law whose students they purportedly are.

The University of Bristol is to be congratulated for having a Intersectional Feminist Society, Ifemsoc for short. In 2018, this charming group proposed a motion to the students' union demanding the trans-exclusionary radical feminist (TERF) groups be barred from holding events in the university. TERFs have been known to deny the new orthodoxy that transwomen are real women, a denial that, in the eyes of the Ifemsoc zealots, amounts to hate speech and endangers so-called trans women. To give the University authorities credit, they've affirmed their stance on free speech but the students' union goes on its own unmerry way. A Committee has been set up to ensure that no student sponsorship of discussions will take place that call trans-activism into question or explores the legal and social implications of transgenderism. I never thought I'd feel sympathy for radical feminists but—wait a minute, no, I still don't feel any sympathy for them. It's fun to see one radical group devour another, especially when the path to glory of the trans activists was cleared by the propaganda and campaigning of radical feminism, a clearance (if I can mix my metaphors) that has now come back to bite them.

21ˢᵗ century academic blasphemy

Just over two hundred years ago, Percy Bysshe Shelley was sent down from Oxford for arguing for the necessity of atheism. You might think, that was then, this is now, so goodbye to all that. Not so. You can still get into trouble for blasphemy at our universities, it's just that the subjects about which one can blaspheme have changed. Transgenderism would appear to be flavour of the year in requiring special protection with almost half of the universities restricting critical discussion of that topic in some way or other. Some, such as the Universities of Leeds Beckett, Newcastle and Imperial prohibit what they see as 'transphobic propaganda' while others, such as the Universities of St Andrews, Sussex and Cardiff are committed to eliminating 'transphobic material' from the curriculum. One wonders what is dealt with in the biology courses in these universities!

Two hundred years on from Shelley's nefarious activities, religious sensibilities are still to be protected, only this time, Christianity is more or less fair game while criticism of other religions will attract opprobrium. (Ask yourself, which religion has the almost exclusive distinction of having the suffix *phobia* attached to it as a standard term of reproach?) Almost half of the universities warn their staff and students against insulting faith groups. A significant difference between Shelley's time and ours is that then it was the university authorities that censored free speech, now it is mainly student groups or the university authorities acting at the behest or in fear of such groups that are the ones that censor. Universities are run today largely by bureaucrats, usually former academics, who appear to value a quiet life above all else and are unwilling to face down the unrepresentative identitarians who infest the students' unions and who regard free speech as a front for the oppression of the marginalised and not a means by which ideas can be expressed and evaluated. Come back, Percy, all is forgiven!

Students are not delicate and fragile flowers who can be irreparably harmed by words or ideas that challenge, disturb or even insult them and they don't need father or mother substitutes to protect them. The writer of the editorial in *The New Criterion* asks, 'What is it about universities that makes them such hothouses of moral incontinence, intellectual stupefaction, and political infantilisation?' (Anon. 2017a) Good question. I wish there were a good answer. Is it that institutions are like fish—when they die, the rot starts in the head and works downwards? Stupidity is not a rare feature of individual and corporate life, but it seems that if you want super-refined and stellar stupidity, you have to go to the institution that is supposed by its very nature to be the producer and conserver of intellectual culture.

The *New Criterion* editorial writer quotes this gem from someone called Inderpal Grewal, who is the Chair of the Women's, Gender, and Sexuality Studies Program at Yale and who writes in a newsletter for the WGSS and the Lesbian, Gay, Bisexual & Transgender Studies Program that 'Misogyny, patriarchy, racism, bigotry, Islamophobia, ableism, transphobia, homophobia, xenophobia: these have emerged as speakable, visible, popular, and powerful themes in public and political discourse in the US.' (see Anon. 2017a) That's pretty bad, Professor Grewal. Tell us what you and the rest of the WGSS/LGBTS gang are going to do about it. Professor Grewal hastens to reassure those of us who might be worried that academic staff at Yale might be attending to their own business instead of busy minding other people's (unless, of course, their business *is* minding other people's business) that 'The WGSS/LGBTS community at Yale stands against all the bigotry and hate that has been expressed during this [2016] election season. We resolve to work toward defending and protecting the communities that are now threatened by the authoritarian, white heteropatriarchy that will be the face of the nation-state, and we refuse to normalize its hateful powers.' I am sure we can all breathe a sigh of relief to know that the massed forces of the WGSS/LGBTS community at Yale are ever vigilant and ready to person the barricades against the evil forces of the white, heteropatriarchy. White, heteropatriarchy, eh? Now, what could that be? White is white, of course. Hetero? Ah yes, people whose sexual inclinations are directed towards people of the other sex. And patriarchy? Well, that's just men. So, the WGSS/LGBTS are ready and willing to take on white, straight men.

It's not just the students who are into restricting speech. Some academics want to get into the game too. In December 2016, in the wake of the traumatic (traumatic to liberals, that is) election of Donald Trump to the US Presidency, a group of twenty four academics at Washington State University wrote a letter to their academic community in which they decried the defence of free speech which, they say, hurts what they described as 'marginalised' students. 'We have,' they said, 'witnessed an increase of exclusionary language based on race, citizenship status and religious affiliation in recent months; here on campus, with the erection of a wall and several other incidents on/off campus and in social media, the everyday realities of racism, xenophobia, and other forms of bigotry have been on full display.' It isn't enough, they said, to encourage open-mindedness and sensitivity (or, as they write it in scare quotes, "open-mindedness" and "sensitivity") for that only leads to a culture that 'accepts and tolerates bigotry and harassment'. Tolerance, too, is not something they're all that keen on (or rather, "tolerance"), likewise discourses of free speech for these, they say, 'undeviatingly create a campus that is especially disempowering to marginalized students.' So, what should be done in place of this feeble insistence on free speech, tolerance, open-mindedness and sensitivity? 'We must,' they told us, 'create a campus that asserts that we are anti-racist, anti-sexist, anti-xenophobia, anti-homophobic, anti-Islamophobic, anti-ableism, and anti-bigotry' by working 'to create mechanisms and structures that combat hate, which empower all constituencies to be active in our collective efforts to rid the campus of bigotry and systemic inequality.'

Mechanisms and structures, eh? I wonder what they have in mind, if they have anything in mind at all, other than the expression of their intolerance for tolerance, their freely-expressed detestation of free speech and a display of minds so open that one suspects that nothing can stay in them for long. An editorial in *The New Criterion* commenting on this egregious piece of cant remarks, 'The modern social justice warrior abominates disagreement as a form of heresy. Accordingly, he rejects tolerance in favor of enforced, indeed totalitarian, conformity. It is the antithesis of what a liberal-arts education was all about, which is why its installation at the center of our erstwhile liberal-arts institutions makes for such a sad irony.' (Anon 2017b; see also Driscoll 2019)

Some students go further than just banning speakers and topics that they do not want to hear, calling into question the very notion of truth itself. 'What is truth?', asked Pilate. It's a myth, say some students from the Claremont Colleges who took issue with an email circulated by the departing President of Pomona College after protests had prevented an invited speaker, Heather McDonald, a critic of Black Lives Matter, from delivering her address. In his email of April 7th 2017, President David W. Oxtoby wrote, 'We remain fully committed to free speech and academic freedom at Pomona College …. Colleges and universities have a unique opportunity and responsibility to bring challenging issues forward for dialogue, even by those with whom we may disagree or whose speech we find offensive. Protest has a legitimate and celebrated place on college campuses. What we cannot support is the act of preventing others from engaging with an invited speaker. Our mission is founded upon the discovery of truth, the collaborative development of knowledge and the betterment of society.'

Nothing too revolutionary there, you might think. Think again. Here's what the students think. First, they have serious doubts about the value of free speech. 'Free speech, a right many freedom movements have fought for, has recently become a tool appropriated by hegemonic institutions. It has not just empowered students from marginalized backgrounds to voice their qualms and criticize aspects of the institution, but it has given those who seek to perpetuate systems of domination a platform to project their bigotry'. So much for free speech. What about truth? Well, truth is pretty much a myth and not a harmless one either.

> Historically, white supremacy has venerated the idea of objectivity, and wielded a dichotomy of 'subjectivity vs. objectivity' as a means of silencing oppressed peoples … The idea that there is a single truth—'the Truth'—is a construct of the Euro-West that is deeply rooted in the Enlightenment, which was a movement that also described Black

and Brown people as both subhuman and impervious to pain. This construction is a myth and white supremacy, imperialism, colonization, capitalism, and the United States of America are all of its progeny. The idea that the truth is an entity for which we must search, in matters that endanger our abilities to exist in open spaces, is an attempt to silence oppressed peoples.

So there! Now you know, or at least you know if you can parse this delightfully daft piece of English prose. What these students are attempting to express in a vulgar and lumpenproletarian way has been presented much more forcefully by such postmodern luminaries as Stanley Fish.

In his *Why There Is No Such Thing as Free Speech: And It's a Good Thing Too* (1994) Fish defends campus speech codes and argues that, since all speech is in fact restricted, in the end, the only issue is one of power. He is unashamedly unprincipled in his advice to campus speech code proponents, counselling them in the following way: 'So long as so-called free-speech principles have been fashioned by your enemy ... contest their relevance to the issue at hand; but if you manage to refashion them in line with your purposes, urge them with a vengeance.' (Fish, 114) While one might commend Fish's critique of free speech fundamentalism, in the end, the irony is that Fish's approach, as with all forms of relativism, is self-stultifying. It uses reason and argument and evidence (or a simulacrum thereof) to persuade us that reason and argument and evidence are merely rhetorical devices to disguise the use of power and, in so doing, cuts the ground out from under its own feet.

Safe spaces

At the opening of the 2016-17 academic year, in a robust defence of the value of free speech, the Dean of Students at the University of Chicago sent a letter to all first year students in which he said that the University did not support trigger warnings, wasn't prepared to cancel invited speakers because what they had to say might be controversial, and did not condone the creation of so-called 'safe spaces' where students could 'retreat from ideas and perspectives at odds with their own.' Needless to say, this letter proved to be controversial. Part of the controversy comes from the term 'safe space' and the reality it is supposed to denote.

From a libertarian perspective, any group, students or otherwise, can make their own arrangements for membership and include or exclude whoever they wish and allow or disallow topics for discussion. People should be free to associate as they wish *and free to dissociate as they wish*. So, may people create safe spaces? Yes, of course, under the principle of freedom of association/dissociation and as long as they do it on their own property. On libertarian principles, you can associate with whomever you please and dissociate from whomever you please for any reason you please, good or bad. If someone want to start a female-only left-handed tiddlywinks club, that, while bizarre, is perfectly in order. If someone wants to set up a group whose members can discuss how repressed and oppressed they are, so be it. But freedom of association and freedom of dissociation has to apply across the board and cannot be selectively applied so that some groups get to decide who they include or exclude while other groups do not. If what's meant by a safe space is the creation of a group to which only certain kinds of people are invited and in which only certain kinds of views can be expressed, there can no objection on libertarian principles to this. One might think it stupid or regressive but if people want to associate with tiddly-winkers and not associate with rugby players, that's their business. If they wish to make use of university property to hold meetings of their group, the university, on the MHMR maxim, has the right to decide whether or not to accede to their request.

But in some of its iterations, the notion of safe space has a larger dimension, literally a larger dimension. Some students and student organisations demand that the university *as a whole* become a safe space from which all ideas and concepts and narratives and histories and theories that challenge their own must be excluded. According to those who hold such views, having a non-platformed speaker come to speak at your university is just like having them in your living room. Except, of course, that it isn't. The university isn't your living room. It isn't any kind of room, and even if it were, it isn't yours. What the demand for a university-wide safe space comes down to is the demand that you and your mates get to determine what other students may or may not hear. This is a kind of student-on-student censorship, a shocking idea to someone who, like myself, is a child of the 60s and 70s. The problem in the university, then, is not with particular groups of students associating or dissociating as they please, but with pressure from activists to turn the entire public, teaching side of the university into a safe space. Lectures cannot be circumscribed in such a way that students are guaranteed not to be presented with ideas that they might find disturbing. In fact, one might go so far as to say that if students aren't intellectually disturbed while at university, the university isn't doing its job!

Whatever about the free association/dissociation of particular individuals, then, the idea that the university as a whole should be a safe space, a place of emotional and intellectual placidity into which no disturbing ideas are permitted to intrude, is totally at odds with the very nature of the university. Of course, the plea to make the university a safe space is often just a thinly disguised attempt to make it a safe space for *my* ideas and *my* opinions but no others, especially my ideas about sexuality, race, and the imminent destruction of the environment by evil capitalists. As the writer of an editorial in *The New Criterion* notes, 'Today, by contrast, a college education, apart from whatever technical or administrative skills it may impart, seems geared to reinforcing a set of intellectual and moral clichés and protecting its charges from confronting any idea that has not received its Good Housekeeping Seal of political correctitude. Enforcing a regimen of intellectual timidity fired by ravenous moral resentment, today's colleges are in fact factories for the production of sclerotic, politically correct conformity on any contentious moral or intellectual issue.' (see Anon. 2016)

Green shoots of resistance

But hold on to your hats, folks, all is not lost! While as recently as 1990, a mere 42 percent of college professors identified as liberal or far-left, by 2014, that figure had approached 60 percent. Meanwhile, only 12 percent of professors identified as conservative. That being so, some students have actually made the case that they would like to have *more* conservative professors on their campus! In the autumn of

2017, an editorial in the Georgetown University campus newspaper *Hoya* argued that the dearth of conservative professors at Georgetown is leaving students unprepared for the intellectual diversity that they are likely to encounter in the real world. They'd like to be prepared for that world when they enter it and would appreciate developing skills in debating and in reasoned argument. The *Hoya* editorial makes a number of reasonable points. First, critical thinking can be developed only where views are challenged and students are exposed to a variety of viewpoints. Second, ideological homogeneity leads to intolerance. And third, ideological uniformity on campus is problematic for all students, not just for conservative students. Liberals students are confirmed in groupthink, and conservative students are alienated. Who are these crazy students who want to hear a range of social and political views? They should be sent to re-education camps, like South Park's Death Camp of Tolerance!

Many university administrators are paragons of pusillanimity when it comes to dealing with the student crybullies. The most spectacular example of this is perhaps what has come to be called the Evergreen State College Affair. In Mike Naynas's documentary on this shameful episode, 'Evergreen academics can be seen meekly and repeatedly submitting to ideological manipulation, and on a number of occasions terrified senior faculty offer transparently insincere professions of faith in the hope of evading the vengeful fury of their mindlessly sloganeering student tormentors.' (Farrington; see Nayna 2019 & 2019a and, if you have a strong stomach, Anon. 2017) By contrast with the craven Evergreen administrators, the President of Ohio State University stands out as a knight in shining armour. He rejected the demands of his own protesters, refused to negotiate with them, informed them that they were in violation of the Student Code of Conduct and that if they didn't clear the building by a set time, the police would be called. In a wonderfully ironic stroke, the reason given for the removal of the students was that they were violating a safe space, the people who worked in the building being intimidated by their presence. How that must have stung!

Louise Richardson, the vice-chancellor of Oxford, said something that deeply offended a lot of people, so much so that over 2,000 sundry students, academics and LGBTQ+ activists have demanded an apology from her. What terrible things did she say? At a *Times Higher Education* (*THE*) summit, she said: 'I've had many conversations with students who say they don't feel comfortable because their professor has expressed views against homosexuality. They don't feel comfortable being in class with someone with those views. And I say, "I'm sorry, but my job isn't to make you feel comfortable. Education is not about being comfortable. I'm interested in making you uncomfortable".' (BBC News 2017) Not only does she say such horrible things but she had the temerity to suggest that those who find the views of others objectionable should—hold your breath— engage with those persons and challenge them! For the apology-demanders, Richardson is an old stick-in-the-mud who thinks a university is a place where the clash of ideas engages and challenges the minds of students whereas our apology-demanders appear to think that universities are seminaries or re-education camps for indoctrinating students in contemporary orthodoxies, especially in inculcating the rejection of the seven contemporary deadly sins of racism, sexism, homophobia, transphobia, misgendering, victim-blaming and cultural appropriation.

Snowflakes and mourning sickness

A little over 20 years ago, Diana, Princess of Wales, came close to being canonised as Britain's first secular saint. The emotional incontinence shockingly displayed at the time of her death indicated that a profound change had taken place in British society and perhaps not only in British society. Diana may have faded from our memories but the social change evinced in the infamous 'outpouring of grief' at her death remains a constituent part of our contemporary culture. The Diana phenomenon ushered in a veritable Age of Aquarius, the valorising of feelings and emotions and the denigration of rationality. Why were all these people, almost every one of whom never knew Diana and, given the different social circles in which they moved, never would have known her, why were they weeping for her? 'What's Diana to them, or they to Diana, that they should weep for her?' The circumstances of her death were objectively no worse and the material circumstances of her life infinitely better than that of the thousands of people who died that same day, but where were the crowds of mourners and the flowers and the cards and the maudlin tears for those who died of starvation or malaria or dysentery, alone, forgotten? The Queen, exemplifying the traditional British values of emotional reserve, was cast as a villain in the piece but who can forget the tremor in Tony Blair's voice? In with feeling, empathy, subjectivity and empty rhetorical gestures—out with reason, argument, evidence, and objectivity. Edgar Jones, professor in the history of medicine and psychiatry at King's College London sees the death of Princess Diana as a moment that signalled a significant shift in British culture. He writes, 'I can remember watching it on television, and as the car left Kensington Palace, you could hear the sound of people wailing—people who had obviously never met Diana, but who were still in tears. It was acceptable to show your emotions.' (Jones 2017) How times have changed. Now we valorise emotions not reason, feelings not argument. Arguments are for the emotionally repressed, the virtuously challenged. What really matters is whether something hurts you, your sense of self or your feelings. Our emotionally expressive age represents a collective regression of adults, in particular young adults, to the status of children.

One term coined to describe this nauseating emotional demonstration was 'mourning sickness'. (The term is not mine, but I wish I had thought of it!) Mourning sickness is just one form of the emotional incontinence that has seized upon contemporary society. It is of a kind with other emotion-centric manifestations such as the breast-beating virtue signalling, the not-in-my-name public demonstrations, the maniacal tearful outbursts of 'Believe her!' during the Brett Kavanaugh hearings and the fulsome apologies for historical wrongs made by those who played no part in them to those who were not injured by them. Rare is the football or rugby match where we don't have a moment's silence for some worthy but previously unknown person. Politicians and police chiefs feel obliged to offer condolences to total strangers for their losses. And whatever happened to the handshake? Now, it seems that the least one can offer to total strangers when you meet them is a hug and a kiss! Where once we might have discussed our problems with our closest friends or our religious advisor, now it seems that we're happy to talk about just about anything on the radio or on TV with little or no sense of reticence or decorum and we confidently expect to be applauded for our bravery in so doing. But isn't it good to express our emotions? Do we really want to go back to the bad old days when we bottled everything up? Well, to use a somewhat crude analogy, I suggest it might be better to risk a little emotional constipation than to suffer from emotional diarrhoea. Yes, of course we must express our emotions—we're not automatons—but there is a time and a place for everything.

It is easy to believe that the emotional distress displayed by the young, particularly (but not only) by students, is simply assumed as a weapon in the culture wars. It would be bad enough if these students were merely simulating indignation or anger as some cynics suspect but the really worrying things is that they really *are* indignant, they really *are* angry! Bizarre as it may seem, their emotional distress is genuine even if unfounded. In many cases, students are no longer perceived or treated as autonomous beings but as vulnerable not-quite-adult elderly children who have their offenceometers always turned up to 11, ever-ready to wilt at a racist joke or fall to pieces at a sexist song lyric.

You might be as surprised as I was to discover that the main purpose of a university is no longer learning but that is what the UK's higher education minister Sam Gyimah told us in 2018 when he called for a greater focus on mental health issues. According to Mr Gyimah, universities must not only provide academic courses but must also provide emotional support for their students in order, he says, to fulfil the university's purpose. It appears that some vice-chancellors, the more traditional of them, believe that the primary purpose of the university is the training of the mind but, Mr Gyimah assures us, this is no longer the case. This is good to know as it seems that not all that much learning appears to go on in universities in any case. Universities should be acting *in loco parentis* the minister tells us which will come as a bit of a shock to those students who thought that for the first time they could get on with their lives without having their parents peeking over their shoulders. Mr Gyimah's pronouncements appear to derive some support from the testimony of Malia Bouattia, the former President of the UK's National Union of Students, who commented in 2016 that going to university in the UK could be psychologically destructive for black students. It appears that incoming students are so infected with innate racist prejudices that some universities hold workshops to help them to acknowledge them and deal with them. Campus racism is everywhere, it seems, from casual conversation in the university's bars to the university curriculum itself. The curriculum is too white, under-stimulating black students who are unable to identify with what they are being taught. There is a wonderful irony here that originally those who opposed racism argued that all should be treated the same whereas now, on campus at least, they are arguing for differential treatment.

Why should we be surprised that the UK's minister for higher education should have this bizarre view of the function of universities when those in charge of them seem to think along the same lines. The *Telegraph* reported (2 May 2019) that Universities UK (UUK), which represents the vice-Chancellors of the universities, published a review that declared that universities would have to become racially diverse and inclusive if BAME (black, Asian, minority and ethnic) students were to succeed academically. Universities should consult with students to ensure that what they teach isn't overly white or Euro-centric. Lady Amos who led UUK's review said the BAME students don't feel as if they belong at university and it seems that the reason for this, or at least part of the reason for this, is that they do not see their experiences or their history reflected in the content of their courses. Ah, I see, and there was I naively thinking that one went to university to be introduced to new and challenging ideas in a stimulating intellectual environment when what is actually desirable is to meet old and familiar intellectual friends. Silly me.

At Manchester University's student union's first union meeting of 2018, the union's Liberation and Access Officer (what a wonderful title!) Sara Khan argued that traditional methods of applause was not sufficiently accessible to all students. The student union resolved to replace audible clapping by jazz hands and to encourage student groups and societies to do the same. Jazz hands were adopted by the National Union of Students (NUS) in 2015 on the basis that clapping triggers anxiety. Critics say such behaviour is typical of what has been called a snowflake generation of students, quick to take offence, intolerant of disagreement and over-sensitive to perceived slights. Some students claim to be psychologically injured by the use of the term *snowflake* to characterise them! There is a perverse but delightful irony in their rejection of this term as a proper description of their mental fragility and, at the same time, their claim that being so described damages their mental health!

All of this is occurring at a time when the Youth Index published by the UK's Prince's Trust tells us that the 'happiness and confidence young people feel in their lives has fallen to their lowest levels since the study was first commissioned in 2009.' Young people in the UK, it seems, 'fear for their emotional health more than ever before, as worries about the future, money and generally "not being good enough" pile up on them and their happiness and confidence in their emotional health has dropped to the lowest levels ever recorded.' (see Prince's Trust 2018) The findings come from an online survey in which a sample of 2,194 16-to-25 year olds participated between 9th and 26th November 2017. What is striking about the report is the mismatch between the experience of those surveyed and the objective facts of their existence. Some of this can be explained by the pathologisation of experience. 'Young people,' the report tells us, 'are particularly worried about their emotional health, which was the area that saw the biggest drop in happiness.' Leaving aside the not unimportant fact that there is no such thing as emotional health except metaphorically, feeling bad or experiencing anxiety or lacking confidence is the normal condition of all people some of the time and many young people most of the time. That said, it doesn't explain why 21 per cent of those surveyed think that their lives will amount to nothing no matter how hard they try or the almost 40% who don't feel in control of their lives. Emily Dinsmore asks, 'Are we witnessing a younger generation uniquely afflicted by hardship, or is something else driving this sense of unease?' She points out the mismatch between appearance and reality, saying, 'by most conventional measures, life for young people today is much better than it was for earlier generations. We are more likely to go to university, we have access to cheap and easy international travel, and developments in healthcare and technology mean we will likely live longer. Even financially we are better off: since 1975, full-time wages have doubled, and a higher proportion of workers are now paid above the minimum wage. The idea that young people have it harder than any previous generation just doesn't stack up. Nor does the idea that young people today are far more affected by mental-health problems than any previous generation.' (Dinsmore 2018)

Here's a modest proposal! If university life is so stressful as to risk damaging the poor students' mental health by requiring them to undertake independent study at the same time as they are having to make new friends and learn to live away from home, why not just get rid of the whole expensive apparatus of lectures, libraries, and all the rest of the academic paraphernalia and just redesign university campuses as playgrounds? Oh wait! Perhaps that has already happened!

To those who wonder where our current generation of 'snowflake' students came from, Brendan O'Neill answers, 'When you watched, or even presided over, the creation over the past 40 years of a vast system of laws and speech codes to punish insulting or damaging words, and the construction of a vast machine of therapeutic intervention into everyday life, what did you think the end result would be?' His point is that the eruption of Safe Spaces and similar nonsense is not some sudden, unexpected phenomenon but the logical result of policies that go back quite a few years. The fragility of (some) contemporary students is linked to the 'relentless rise of the therapeutic outlook.' (O'Neill 2015) Today's students are weak, fragile, frail and easily damaged and they may well be if that's how they've been taught to be by their parents and their parents' generation.

James L. Nolan Jr, the author of *The Therapeutic State*, was interviewed by Ella Whelan, an assistant editor at *Spiked*. He noted that 'In the aftermath of Donald Trump's election victory in the US, there were numerous protests. At one of the colleges where students were protesting, they were carrying signs that demanded the school's administration provide more therapists for students, as though this was the answer to the outcome of the election: "We need more therapy!" This is an example of the way in which society invites a therapeutic intervention, not just the state adopting a therapeutic perspective to expand its authority.' (Whelan 2017)

The extreme and abnormal sensitivity shown by some students to what they deem violence seems to be effectively restricted to those who were born after 1995, that is, to those who have grown up with social media and may be regarded as digital natives, the i-gen or the internet generation. The psychologist Jonathan Haidt thinks the susceptibility of the i-gen to extreme sensitivity has three main causes: social media, rising national polarisation, and the decline in unsupervised (adult-free) time during childhood. Of these three causes, I consider the first to be the most significant. It is becoming reasonably clear that social media are agents of pathologised sensitivity. Facebook and Twitter act as powerful amplifying devices to intensify an already dangerously neurotic emotional atmosphere. Now it takes less and less to arouse anger (whether real or simulated) than ever before and almost no energy at all to blast it into hyperspace. Offence must never be given by anybody to anybody, feelings must never be hurt, no matter if speech has to be restricted or prohibited or baseless accusations made against the innocent.

What I have elsewhere called 'the literalisation of metaphor' is what happens when a concept such as violence, which primarily means a physical interference with another's bodily integrity, is taken to apply literally to words or attitudes. Haidt writes, 'When a word like "violence" is allowed to creep so that it includes a lot of things that are not violence, then this causes a cascade of bad effects. It's bad for the students themselves because they now perceive an idea that they dislike, or a speaker that they dislike, as having committed a much graver offence against themselves—which means that they will perceive more victimisation of themselves.' A punch in the face is an act of violence; being told you're an idiot is not an act of violence, except metaphorically. It's unpleasant, of course, even if it is warranted by your stupidity.

Two aspects of social media are worth noting; anonymity and the effectively costless nature of their use. Whereas in earlier times, if you wanted to abuse a total stranger and you weren't in their immediate presence, you would have had to write a letter or make a phone call. You would have had to take *some* trouble or incur *some* cost. Now, that cost or trouble has effectively diminished to vanishing point. (see Nagle, passim) This has had the effect of producing volumes of ill-thought out and unreflective effusions. In the pre-internet age, I once spoke to an editor of one of Ireland's leading daily papers about a series he was running. I asked him what kind of reaction he had been getting and he said, 'Fantastic. We had ten letters to the editor on the subject.' *Ten* letters! Ah yes, innocent days! In addition to the financial and time cost factors which dampened the volume of transactions while improving their quality, if you wanted to engage with another person in the pre-social-media age you ran the risk of a possible physical encounter which caused most people to moderate their mode of expression in the interests of self-protection if not politeness. This no longer holds. On social media, people think of themselves as living in a protected electronic bubble. Just as people wouldn't dream of picking their noses in public view but do so freely when sitting in their cars in traffic as if they couldn't be seen, so too, the social media bubble of anonymity creates an electronic *Get Smart*-like cone of invisibility akin to Gyges Ring or H. G. Wells' invisible man. The pre-social-media age has seen the erosion of politeness, first on electronic media and latterly its export to the arena of normal social intercourse. It's now apparently acceptable for students to scream at professors who are deemed not to be sufficiently woke (*woke* is the in-term for the hyperbolically socially aware!). If you search online, you can see video clips of Yale students screaming at a professor who had the temerity to suggest that Halloween costumes should not be policed for offensiveness.

The i-gen is one of the most protected generations of children ever. Guarded constantly by helicoptering parents, driven everywhere, supervised at all times, never allowed to do anything remotely dangerous or, God forbid, on their own. This is the social equivalent of not allowing your children to be exposed to dirt so that their immune system never develops properly. Similarly, by being protected from all instances of social 'dirt', this generation has failed to develop the social and psychological antibodies that would enable them to function in normal society. Their social personas are anti-fragile, to use Nassim Taleb's term, and lack the challenges and pressure they require if they are to function efficiently. Haidt writes,

Kids need conflict, insult, exclusion—they need to experience these things thousands of times when they're young in order to develop into psychologically mature adults. Every adult has to learn to handle these things and not get upset, especially by minor instances. But in the name of protecting our children we have deprived them of the unsupervised time they need to learn how to navigate conflict among themselves. That is one of the main reasons why kids and even university students today find words, ideas and social situations more intolerable than those same words, ideas and situations would have been for previous generations of students.

Haidt identifies three very bad ideas that are not helping students to flourish. First is the idea that their feelings are always right. Reason out; feelings in. If it feels good, it must be right; if it feels bad, it's wrong. Argument is a form of intellectual aggression and the demand for evidence is an insult to my feelings. The second bad idea that Haidt identifies is that what doesn't kill you just makes you weaker. This is a denial of the anti-fragile nature of our social and psychological lives. And the third bad idea is that the world is divided not just into those who are right (those who agree with us) and those who are wrong (those who disagree with us) but into those who are good (those who agree with us) and those who are evil (those who disagree with us).

Emotional incontinence has even started to contaminate practical politics, an area of life that used to be characterised by vigorous and robust verbal rough-and-tumble. In March 2018, Frank Furedi wrote, 'The accusation that a public figure behaved inappropriately towards another person carries incredible weight. So much authority does such an accusation carry that individuals are far more likely to quit if accused of bullying or another form of inappropriate behaviour than if found guilty of incompetence or administrative failure.' (Furedi 2018) How prescient was that comment! How Furedi must feel vindicated by the trial by emotional accusation of Brett Kavanaugh in the news media of the USA.

Claim and counterclaim of inappropriate behaviour fly about. When the Labour MP Debbie Abrahams was forced out her shadow cabinet position because of claims about her behaviour towards her staff, her response was to make a counter-claim of victimisation by bullying! To call the 'culture of bullying' into question is to commit yet another sin, the sin of insensitivity. All of this nonsense parallels the meta-discourse strategy in public discussions where it is no longer so much the truth or cogency of what you say that matters but, rather, how you say whatever it is you say, especially if your saying of it is deemed to be offensive, hurtful, or aggressive. If the topic of discussion can be shifted to the meta-level of feelings, there is no need to pay attention to the argument. Once upon a time and not so very long ago, to be a victim was to be someone who was weak and deserved pity. Now, to be a victim is to establish a pre-emptive claim on a moral (and often a legal) status that is empowering. This is especially characteristic of today's identity politics where various groups compete in an unseemly competition to establish who among the legion of victims is the most victimised. The payoff is not pity but tangible goods such as money (via compensation) or privilege (entry to jobs or universities otherwise unattainable).

To conclude, let's return to our students. Reeding Aeschylus, Plato and Herodotus, and studying Ancient Greece, Rome and Egypt is, it seems, racist. The first word in the previous sentence is not a typo, for it is in Reed College in Oregon that students are forced—dear God is there no end to the tyranny they have to endure!—to think about what these ancient white men said *sooooo* long ago. Some students expressed their displeasure by sitting in the front row with their mouths taped up. There may be some among my more cynical readers who think that this is a practice that could be more widely adopted for quite a large number of students and for considerably longer periods of time—say between the ages of 18 to 29—but let us not indulge these cynics. If our Reedies don't want Classical thought, what do they want? Well, apart from not having their minds contaminated by the bearded old men of Greece, Rome and Egypt, they want to play a bigger role in appraising faculty and, wait for it, mandatory racial sensitivity training. Of course, these idiot students (I use the term *idiot* advisedly—students should know the etymology of the term) seem to be unaware (well, how could they be aware, they don't know anything!) that Western civilisation, based on Greek, Roman and Judaeo-Christian thought has been the principal tool for the overturning of oppression.

The Reed administration's response was, as is now customary, pusillanimous. Instead of promptly expelling these brats, the college tolerated silent protest but not active disruption. But, as is usual in these cases, tolerance was taken to be evidence of weakness and the students described the College as racist and white supremacist. In a bold move, they said that at Reed, 'Dissent will NOT be tolerated when crusty old white professors get upset about the prospect of having to attend ... diversity training'. As a very crusty, very old and very white professor myself (let's ignore the students' racism and ageism for the moment) I'm not unnaturally a little disturbed by the students' cavalier attitude. But there is hope. Not all the protestors' fellow students were entranced by their activities. In one instance, a black student objected to the disruption of his class caused by Black Lives Matter protesters and his intervention was met with applause by other members of his class.

It was once said that at a meeting of the bishops' conference in a certain country (which shall be nameless) a shiver ran around the room looking for a spine to run up. Much the same could be said for any collectivity of academics. Will the academics at Reed and at other universities where much the same nonsense has gone on, develop a spine and fight back?

❧

Tolerance is Intolerable

Tolerance—the disposition to be patient with or indulgent to the opinions or practices of others.
—*Oxford English Dictionary*

Tolerance: intellectual and practical

In the first part of this book, I argued that the foundational principle of libertarianism, the Zero Aggression Principle (ZAP) implied the 'My House, My Rules' (MHMR) maxim for free speech, a maxim that is at once permissive and restrictive. It is permissive in that it allows you to say anything you please about anything or anyone using your own property or the property of others (with their permission) but it is restrictive inasmuch as others are under no obligation (apart from contract) to put their property at your disposal. Any method of controlling or limiting speech that does not violate the ZAP—persuasion, moral reprobation, norms of politeness or etiquette, and so on—may be used as people consider appropriate.

What does the ZAP imply about toleration? Given that the ZAP tells us that we are entitled to use force or have others use force on our behalf only to defend ourselves against aggression, that means that if others have beliefs that we think are false, or if they engage in actions that we find mildly distasteful or reprehensible or even repulsive, we are not entitled to use force to prevent them believing or acting as they do unless their beliefs or actions constitute aggression. As is the case with speech, methods of limitation or control that do not violate the ZAP may be used as may be appropriate.

There are at least two kinds of tolerance: *intellectual tolerance* (and its corollary, intellectual *in*tolerance) and *practical tolerance* (and its corollary, practical *in*tolerance). Failure to appreciate this distinction can lead to a lot of heat and very little light.

If you hold that a proposition is true, then, of necessity, you must deny truth to the propositions that are contrary to it or contradictory to it. This is *intellectual intolerance*. If, for example, you believe it to be true that all philosophers are superbly intelligent, then you cannot hold as true the proposition that no philosophers are superbly intelligent (its contrary) or the proposition that some philosophers are not superbly intelligent (its contradictory). The consequence of holding any beliefs at all—*any* beliefs, not just controversial beliefs in religion or politics—is that one is logically committed to denying their contraries and contradictories or any beliefs that logically imply their contraries or contradictories. If I believe that 2+2 = 4, then I must reject the belief that 2+2 = 5 or 3.927 or any beliefs that logically imply that 2 + 2 = 5 or 3.927. If I believe that God created the universe and everything in it, then I must reject the belief that the universe can be completely explained naturalistically. Naturalists, on the other hand, must reject all forms of belief that imply the existence of a supernatural order. A Buddhist has to reject the idea of a transcendent deity common to all forms of monotheism. A Christian must reject the truth of those beliefs in other religions that are contradictory or contrary to his Christian beliefs and *vice versa*. Intellectual intolerance is mutual, not unidirectional. *All* beliefs or systems of beliefs, whether secular or religious, have this character of intellectual intolerance.

It doesn't follow, however, from the mutual intellectual intolerance of contrary or contradictory beliefs that one is thereby committed to persecuting or prosecuting those who hold those beliefs and who act on them. Being prepared to live with others who hold beliefs that are inconsistent with ours or who engage in practices that we locate on a spectrum from the mildly objectionable to disgusting is a matter of *practical tolerance*. Intellectual intolerance doesn't necessarily carry with it any particular emotional charge. We are not obliged to hate or fear or despise those who hold beliefs that are contrary or contradictory to ours. We may in fact do so but we do not have to do so. We may simply be indifferent to those others or perhaps even pity their intellectual benightedness. But whatever one's emotional attitude to those others, one cannot, in the name of practical tolerance, hold that their beliefs and yours, where those beliefs are mutually exclusive, are simultaneously true. To do so is simply incoherent.

Beliefs are one thing, actions another, although the borders between them can sometimes be difficult to discern. Another's beliefs just as such are unlikely to interfere with mine or limit the range of activities open to me but beliefs often demand practical expression and thus the possibility of practical conflict becomes a reality. It is not difficult to live with the fact that in some matters, other people believe very differently from us but when those beliefs impinge on our range of actions or even, in the extreme, on our ability to hold or express our own beliefs then matters become more difficult.

The justifiable demand for the practical tolerance of the beliefs or actions of others has a tendency to creep towards an entirely unjustifiable demand for some other attitude, such as respect, where respect requires one to esteem or honour or otherwise validate another's beliefs. Toleration, of course, requires no such valida-tion and, indeed, is functionally inconsistent with it, for we do not tolerate that which we agree with or like or respect but that which we believe to be false or misguided or even repulsive. We can see this conceptual creep in full flight in the UNESCO definition of tolerance, which is that it is 'the respect, acceptance and appreci-ation of the rich diversity of our world's cultures....' To which one can only reply, no, it isn't! Tolerance is tolerance; and respect, acceptance and appreciation are, respectively, respect, acceptance and appreciation. Frank Furedi, whose book-length treatment of the concept of tolerance should be required reading (see Furedi 2011a) gives the following definition of tolerance which I am happy to adopt: 'Tolerance affirms the freedom of conscience and individual autonomy. As long as an act does not violate a person's moral autonomy and harm others, tolerance also calls for the absence of constraint on behaviour linked to the exercise of individ-ual autonomy.' (Furedi 2011a, 5) He says elsewhere, 'tolerance ... demands that we accept the right of people to live according to beliefs and opinions that are different, sometimes antithetical, to ours. Tolerance does not invite us to accept or celebrate other people's sentiments, but requires that we live with them and desist from interfering or forcing others to fall in line with our own views.' (Furedi 2012, 32) Peter Wood sums the matter up neatly when he writes, '[I]s demanding "respect" for eccentric views really what we owe other people by way of tolerance? What we owe—most of the time—is non-interference. Respect should not be issued automatically on the premise that all cultural differences deserve it. Some do, some don't. Respect should be reserved for those ideas and cultural attainments in which we discover real worthiness.' (Wood 2003, 220) To sum up, then, we tolerate what we do not believe or do not like, what we find repulsive or disgusting or mildly objectionable.

Because tolerance necessarily implies a negative judgement by A in respect of B's beliefs or practices, it has increasingly come to be seen as objectionable; tolerance, it seems, has become intolerable! For our ideologues, tolerance of difference is not enough. We must defer to others and celebrate their differences but of course, not *all* differences, only the privileged ones. The UNESCO conception of tolerance is, in a curious way, a denial of those very differences that make a difference. When we shift from the standard idea of tolerance as the non-interference with and non-suppression of beliefs and practices that one finds objectionable to the UNESCO idea of tolerance as acceptance, respect and appreciation, it is likely that we do so because we have come to the conclusion that none of these beliefs or practices matter very much. But if there is one thing more irritating than being tolerated it is not being taken seriously! Furedi again: 'reflecting on our difference with others' points of view, letting them know where we stand and what we find disagreeable in their opinions, is the very stuff of a vibrant democracy. Without it tolerance turns into shallow indifference, an excuse for switching off when others talk.' (Furedi 2011b)

To balance Furedi's masterly academic treatment of the concept of tolerance, The *South Park* episode 'The Death Camp of Tolerance' (S6E14) should be required viewing for anyone who wants to see some essential points about tolerance made in a lighter (and more amusing) vein. In this episode, Mr Garrison, the gay Kindergarten teacher, is offered promotion to Fourth Grade teacher. The Principal of the School inadvertently lets it slip that if the School were to fire Garrison for his being gay, he could sue them for millions. This revelation interests Garrison strangely! He devises a cunning plan. He will behave outrageously, get fired, and then sue the School for wrongful dismissal. Despite his best (worst?) efforts, all that he earns is not dismissal but the Courageous Teacher Award! At the Awards Ceremony at the Museum of Tolerance, he is unable to tolerate the sponginess of the liberal mind and says, 'God-dammit, don't you people get it?! I'm trying to get fired here ... Look, this kind of behavior should not be acceptable from a teacher!' 'But,' the parents protest, 'the Museum tells us to be tolerant.' 'Tolerant, but not stupid!' replies Garrison. 'Look, just because you have to tolerate something doesn't mean you have to approve of it! If you had to like it, it'd be called the Museum of Acceptance! "Tolerate" means you're just putting up with it! You tolerate a crying child sitting next to you on the airplane or you tolerate a bad cold. It can still piss you off!' For this plain speaking, he's convicted of not being tolerant of his own behaviour!

Limits to Tolerance?

Are there any limitations to what one can tolerate? Can others do anything at all that they like, say anything at all that they wish, in any and all circumstances? Clearly not! What, then, are the constraints that should operate to limit one's actions? Here, people differ. Some people would grant society at large through the State (regarded as society's organ of administration) the power to determine what should and what shouldn't be tolerated. This is problematic, not least because there is no guarantee that those who control the levers of power will make their policies on the basis of any morally defensible principle. If the state adopts this role, then various parties in the state will engage in contestation to control the process and to the victor will go the spoils. Much of the controversy surrounding free speech, for example, derives from the dispute over who may and who may not use what are deemed to be public spaces and who gets to set the rules for their use.

The libertarian approach to this problem is one of principle, especially when compared to the hodge-podge of pragmatism that is commonly employed and is, as one might expect, maximally liberal. A person may believe whatever he wishes to believe and give

practical effect to those beliefs in speech or action provided that in
so doing he does not violate the Zero Aggression Principle (ZAP),
that is, provided he does not aggress or threaten to aggress against
the person or property of another. This, while throwing up some
inevitable but not insuperable boundary problems, is less prone
to grant legitimacy to unacceptable limitations on actions and
speech. Another's actions, including the expression of his beliefs,
are however also subject to the rubric of MHMR. This means that
while there are no limitations other than the ZAP to what a person
may believe or do on his own property or on the property of others
with the permission of the property owner, he has no right to use
the property of others without their consent. This, as we have seen,
has consequences for our ability to speak freely.

It might be objected that if the libertarian principle were to be
adopted, the result would be a free-for-all in which a person could
say anything to anyone at any time without fear of consequen
ces. But this is to fall prey to the fallacy that the only effective
sanctions on speech and conduct are legal sanctions. That is not
so. You are not called upon when walking down Oxford Street, if
you should come across someone weighing 500 pounds, to walk up
to him and say, 'My God, you're disgustingly fat!' Such matters are
controlled by informal social norms which are more extensive and
more effective than we often give them credit for being, as indeed
is the case with most of the things that we say and do. Calumny
is the moral offence of publishing what we know to be false and
detrimental about others or of being reckless as to its truth; detraction is the moral offence of publishing what we know to be true
and detrimental to others where one has no moral obligation to
publish such truths. In addition to these moral restrictions, most of
us are trained by our upbringing to avoid giving gratuitous offence
to others. Without these moral and social constraints, it would
scarcely be possible to organise a functioning society even with the
most extensive and minute legal regulations.

In his *On Liberty*, John Stuart Mill was much more concerned
about the effects of informal social constraints on liberty than about
explicit state censorship and he had a point. Social norms, while
effective and necessary, can be carried to extremes and where one

is engaged in a serious discussion with others on serious matters, there is a duty to speak the truth, even if such speaking causes offence. Furedi writes, 'Moral autonomy involves not just self-determination but a willingness to respect others' capacity for autonomous behaviour. This requires an assumption that all the parties to a debate or dialogue have freedom to say what best expresses their inclinations and beliefs. In such conversation, the different parties do not confine their communications to a polite exchange of opinion. Precisely because they take their opinions seriously, views will be expressed with force and will not be self-censored to spare the feelings of others.' (Furedi 2011a, 154) If informal social norms become institutionally politicised and given legal effect, as seems to be increasingly the case, the result will be the paralysis of free speech.

Every age witnesses the re-emergence of heresy in new and interesting forms, for every society tends to have beliefs, doctrines and practices that are taboo. These can be, and often are, the subject of forms of social, and sometimes legal, intolerance. To the extent that a society at large holds certain beliefs to be unquestionable, to that extent the denial of or the expression of a sceptical attitude towards those beliefs tends to provoke active intolerance, usually in the form of the limitation or repression of free speech. To those who are not persuaded of the intrinsic merits of free speech, latter-day heretics or contrarians such as climate change deniers, religious fundamentalists, defenders of hate speech and the like, all require therapeutic intervention and corrective education and, if need be, punishment. Just as religious heretics were to be eliminated as a danger to the one true religion, so modern heretics are to be repressed, denied platforms, fired from their jobs and perhaps even imprisoned. We currently have laws in certain jurisdictions against Holocaust denial and Armenian genocide denial! Will we soon have laws against 'global warming' denial? This isn't a fantasy. Ed Milliband, as the UK's Secretary of State for Energy and Climate Change, once remarked that what the climate change sceptics are saying is 'profoundly dangerous', and an Australian journalist has suggested that we might want to consider imposing criminal sanctions on climate change deniers because denying climate change is, according to him, a crime against humanity, these deniers being clearly dishonest, malevolent, greedy, corrupt and in the pay of big bad corporations.

Tolerance is definitely not the flavour of the age in the new world of supremacy of feelings. If what you say bothers Taysia and causes her bad feelings, then you must be prevented from saying it. Social and moral norms used to act as a means of filtering and dampening various forms of hostility while allowing for real diversity in thought and action but now, those who think differently from Taysia are not just wrong and to be ignored or pitied but are evil and to be repressed.

In contemporary societies, tolerance increasingly comes into focus when it comes to decide whether or not, or to what extent, we should limit people's freedom to speak. Furedi writes, 'In controversies the surround tolerance, it is frequently suggested that it is morally legitimate to curb speech that is offensive or that insults an individual or a group. Time and again there are calls to punish people for disrespecting a culture, insulting a group, or offending an individual. What is overlooked is that freedom of speech requires the expression of opinions which some deem insulting and hurtful.' (Furedi 2011a, 112)

The New (Religious) Intolerance

Writing about what she calls 'The New Intolerance' in the context of the repression of Christians, Mary Eberstadt identifies its four characteristics. (Eberstadt 2015) First, the new intolerance isn't just a Christian problem though it is a particular problem for Christians; it's a problem for everybody. Practicing Christians who refuse to recant are on the front lines of the new intolerance today but where they stand now others will stand in the future. Second, the new intolerance is different from its predecessors. It's largely a matter of the use of intimidation, humiliation and censorship to punish those who dare to think differently, and the object of secular scorn and hatred is not primarily Christian metaphysics or its doctrine of God but its teachings on sex and sexuality. Third, the new form of intolerance is dangerous not only because it is a matter of censorship but even more so because it promotes and encourages self-censorship, even *within* Christian churches which are called by their very constitution not to be conformed to the world. Efforts by Christian Churches to adapt to the new normative environment have led only to more demands for Christian conformism and to the abandonment of actual Christian moral teaching. And finally, brazenly, and with supreme impudence, the new intolerance claims to occupy the moral high ground, while at the same time undermining the religious, moral, social and economic fabric of society.

In parts of the world today, being a Christian can cost you your life. (see Davies; Eberstadt; Shortt; Smith) In the urbane West, you're not likely to be killed for being a Christian, at least, not yet, but it can cost you your job, your friends, your place in a university course and sometimes you may end up as a guest of Her Majesty's government. This form of intolerance is what the Pope has termed 'polite persecution' and it is a phenomenon we can confidently expect to become more and more common.

John Bursch, formerly Michigan's solicitor general, was a legal representative for Steve Tennes and Country Mill Farms in their litigation against the city of East Lansing. Why should that be of interest to anyone? Well, it turns out that Mr Tennes owns Country Mill Farms which regularly sells its produce at the East Lansing Farmer's Market. Up to 2016, Country Mills Farm was not only a regular vendor at the Market but one valued by the city which recognised it as an 'invitational vendor' because of its exceptional service. So what changed in 2016? In 2016, Mr Tennes posted on Facebook that he adhered to the teaching of the Catholic Church that marriage is a sacred union between one man and one woman. He also, as it happens, adheres to the Church's teaching that human beings are made in the image and likeness of God and so have a dignity that must be respected. Nothing particularly radical there, you might think, but Mr Tennes's expression of his orthodox Catholic beliefs was too much for the East Lansing city authorities. He was told to stay away from the Market because there might be protests. He turned up at the Market as usual and there were no protests. So then the City excluded Country Mill Farms because it allegedly violated a city ordinance prohibiting discrimination based on sexual orientation but, of course, Country Mill Farms doesn't discriminate between its customers and its employees on that ground. The City then barred the Market's Planning Committee from inviting Mr Tennes's enterprise to exhibit and demanded that the Committee send an ordinary application from Mr Tennes to it if he should submit one. He did, the Committee did, and the City rejected his application unless and until he should change his religious beliefs and his expression of them. So, Mr Tennes sought an injunction requiring the City to allow him to participate in the Market and the Court, in September 2017, granted the injunction. The City denies it rejected Mr Tennes's application on the grounds of his beliefs but the Court didn't accept that argument. The story continues.

Anti-Catholicism would seem to be one of the last remaining acceptable forms of bigotry. Jacob Rees-Mogg was publicly savaged when he had the temerity to express his Catholic beliefs in public on television. Marriage is a sacrament, he said, and abortion is wrong. What? Cretin! Bigot! How can somebody with these reactionary views have a place in politics or in any decent society? Not so long ago, Catholics in Britain were suspected of owing obedience to a foreign political power and so, it was believed, couldn't be loyal subjects of the monarch. Now, their moral beliefs render them unfit for political office. This is all somewhat puzzling inasmuch as Rees-Mogg has explicitly made it clear that his beliefs are very unlikely to be instantiated in politics and law as the majority of citizens do not agree with him. Nevertheless, in thinking what he does, he's guilty of thought-crime. It's interesting by the way that Muslims who hold views in many areas that are not all that different from those of Rees-Mogg don't seem to attract quite the same degree of public vituperation.

A Catholic student group at Georgetown University called Love Saxa was accused by pro-choice activists of promoting hatred and intolerance. Goodness me! What terrible things had they said or done? Had they advocated lynching blacks—excuse me, people of colour? Incarcerating adulterers? Banning the expression of 'liberal' views. No! They had—wait for it—advocated a traditional view of marriage! Can you imagine that? A Catholic group in a Catholic university expressing Catholic views! How shocking! Such views are hateful, according to the student who submitted a complaint to the University's Dean for Student Engagement. By supporting the idea that marriage is a monogamous and permanent union between a man and a woman, which is the Catholic Church's definition of marriage, this ghastly group had—sharp intake of breath—infringed on the rights of the LGBT community. Some might think that the action of the complainant should rather be considered the kind of attitude that promotes hatred and intolerance but that surely couldn't be right!

The new intolerance is happy to put butchers, bakers and candlestick makers on trial for refusing to give up their religious beliefs. All right, I made up that bit about candlestick makers and butchers but, as we saw, bakers in both the UK and the USA have come under legal attack for their refusal to compromise their beliefs. The new intolerance is happy to threaten those pastors with legal consequences who speak about the sinfulness of homosexuality or the idiocy of gay marriage, even though in those halcyon but long gone days when they used to point out the sinfulness of divorce, no union of gay divorcees rose up to threaten them with legal sanctions.

In 2017, Felix Ngole was ejected from the degree course in social work he was pursuing at Sheffield University because of views he expressed on Facebook to the effect that homosexuality was a sin and same-sex marriage morally unacceptable. The University, applying the standards of the Health and Care Professions Council (HCPC) and having interrogated Mr Ngole, decided that he had failed to show high enough standards of conduct and had also failed to accept that his Facebook musings might damage confidence in the social-work profession. One wonders just how much confidence there *is* in the social-work profession to actually damage but let's leave that to one side. Andrew Tettenborn remarked that 'the university's attitude (which the HCPC seemed to share) was that it could prevent a student reading for a professional qualification from expressing any opinion in public, however lawful, on the basis that it might be perceived by someone somewhere in a way adverse to the profession concerned. This essentially allows the university to suppress any statement by any student on any professional course.' Who is to judge what is and what isn't going to be seen by some random internet browser as being adverse to the social work profession? Andrew Tettenborn again: 'Suppose Mr Ngole had expressed equally strong views in *favour* of same-sex marriage, which someone might have read as calling into question his ability to do social work with, say, pious Muslims. Would the university have acted in the same way? Possibly. But it seems unlikely.' (Tettenborn 2017) In a related incident, Jamie Doward reported that 'A psychologist who has played a key role in opposing the introduction of relationship and sex education lessons in schools is being investigated by her profession's governing body over her fitness to practise.' The National Secular Society wrote to the Health and Care Professions Council (HCPC) to ask if Dr Kate Godfrey-Gausset's views on homosexuality were compatible with the Council's standards. Dr Godfrey-Gausset made the point that 'It is well known that if you speak out against the secular narrative they will silence you through smear campaigns and getting you struck off professionally.' (Doward 2019)

Moral triumphalism

I came across a piece in *The Nation* and I laughed heartily at what I took to be a diabolically clever piece of satire. Then, it was revealed to me that *The Nation* is, apparently, the most widely read weekly journal of progressive political and cultural news, opinion, and analysis and that the piece wasn't meant to be satirical at all! Someone calling herself 'Not a Fan of Social Darwinism' (hereafter NAF) wrote to *The Nation*'s advice columnist, Liza Featherstone, seeking some relationship advice. (Featherstone 2018) 'Dear Liza,' NAF writes, 'I fell into an instant and deep connection with a man while on a work trip. I'm happily married, so there's no chance of a romantic future, but the friendship has been, and is, enlivening. We share many interests, but mostly we have an easy understanding—something slow and patient and unusual in this world. We occasionally talk on the phone about life, and we're looking forward to having lunch when our paths cross again next month.'

Well, so far, so good, apart from possibly flirting with an occasion of sin (adultery). But, leaving that serpent to one side as it doesn't seem to bother NAF, there's yet another snake in this Garden of Eden. NAF continues: 'However, in the gaps between conversations, I've come to realize that he might be a fan of Jordan Peterson. He hasn't mentioned his name, but there have been significant clues. More alarmingly, he has betrayed a thin-skinnedness around sensitive topics like #MeToo and transgender issues. He's said nothing that's outright offensive—maybe because I've made my politics clear. But if I ask directly, and he responds affirmatively that he is a fan of Peterson, what should I do?'

Well, you might think, given the easy understanding that supposedly exists between NAF and her male friend (MF), that our advice columnist will perhaps suggest to NAF that she might consider finding out what MF *actually* thinks (after all, one could be sensitive around #MeToo and transgender issues without necessarily being a Jordan Peterson fan) and broadmindedly explore the issues between them, if, indeed, there are issues between them because, you know, that's what friends with an easy understanding relationship tend to do. Ms Featherstone goes part of the way along this sensible path, suggesting that NAF and MF are lucky to have this understanding relationship even though their values might be somewhat at odds, because closeting oneself away in thought-bubbles is a recipe for becoming intellectually soft and losing the empathy that's essential to persuasion. So far, so good. But then the mask drops. Let me give you Ms Featherstone's own words. 'I'm delighted you plan to keep your clothes on,' she writes, 'not only because you're happily married, but also because it would be advice-columnist malpractice to condone sex with a Jordan Peterson fan.'

Whoa! Where did *that* come from? Why is a (possible) JP fan ruled out of court as a possible enlivening friend in this summary fashion? Because, it seems, Peterson's ideas are repellent (no mention of what these repellent ideas actually are except a hint that they might concern biological determinism) and he has a far-right political agenda, far-right apparently being code for any political philosophy to the dexterous side of Bernie Sanders. If MF *is* a Peterson fan, Ms Featherstone suggests, perhaps it's because he's depressed and lonely. Why would she think this? Because, she says, 'Even more than rage, transphobia, or misogyny, the affect most palpable in Peterson's public appearances is melancholy'. So what, concretely, might NAF do? Outside and apart from any political discussion which the naïve among us might think is what NAF and MF should explore together, Ms Featherstone proposes that NAF might want to suggest that MF 'seek treatment for depression, or at least spend less time on YouTube, which can be a cesspool of self-reinforcing masculine ailments and symptoms.' Well, acting on that advice should bring the relationship between NAF and MF to a shuddering halt. At least it would if I were MF and I were treated in this appallingly patronising and condescending way.

The Intolerant University

What of that bastion of free speech, free thinking and toleration, the university? In the distant days of 2015, a poll of 800 students from across a range of US campuses was conducted to ascertain their attitude towards free speech and, in particular, free speech on campus. For lovers of freedom the results were depressing and it's unlikely that matters have improved in the interim. Just over half the students (51%) were in favour of speech codes regulating the speech of staff and students. Almost two thirds (63%) were fans of trigger warnings to ensure that students wouldn't be intellectually disturbed. And here's the really shocking part. One third of the students polled—and these are all students who've been through at least fourteen years of schooling—when asked to identify the part of the Constitution dealing with free speech couldn't put their finger on the First Amendment! One third, in a hissy-fit of chronological snobbery, thought the First Amendment to be outdated and another third thought that it didn't protect 'hate speech'.

Peter W. Wood, author of the must-read classic *Diversity*, published a piece on what he calls the seven types of suppression of free speech that routinely take place on US campuses and,

I should add, not just on campuses in the US. (Wood 2017) These seven little intellectual dwarves can be handily remembered by the mnemonic created by their initials—O-U-T-R-A-G-E. I've adopted and adapted Wood's schema thus:

O: ostracise dissenters from PC orthodoxy
Disinvite any controversial (that is, conservative or libertarian) speakers; better still, don't invite them in the first place. If, despite your best efforts, one succeeds in coming, disrupt the event or threaten such disorder that the university will cancel the event for health and safety reasons.

U: usurp the curriculum
Work to eliminate all courses that run counter to the new normative environment. In particular, make sure nothing that could possibly be seen as a validation of Western Civilisation makes it onto the curriculum. If such courses are already there, get rid of them.

T: train students to be activists
Turn your courses into advocacy programmes. Train your students to mistake feelings of outrage and indignation for learning and to think that the goal of a university education is transformation; not, of course, transformation of themselves but of those benighted others and the 'system' as a whole in the interests of 'social justice'. Train your students to be on the lookout for anything—a word, a speech, a course, a university policy, an incident of bias (real or imagined), a hate crime (real or imagined)—that can be the occasion for a staged emergency or a planned panic.

R: repress topics deemed unfit for discussion
Preventing wrong ideas from being heard is good but it's not enough; it is much better to prevent them from ever being thought. Anyone expressing doubt as to the correctness of favoured doctrines, for example, the existence of campus rape culture, is to be castigated for defending rapists and victim-blaming. These articles of faith are off-limits to reasonable inquiry and exempt from the requirement to possess evidential support.

A: aggress against the old order and those who uphold it
Those who refuse to 'get with the (social justice) programme' actively
must not be allowed to rest in peace and just get on with their studies
and with their lives. They must be subjected to diversity training or
sexual harassment training and other forms of psychological manipulation. Any form of resistance to this institutional aggression is to be
regarded as micro-aggression and dealt with severely.

G: group people by race, sex and ethnicity
Identity is all. Everything is a matter of which group or groups you
(or your enemies) belong to. Argument and evidence matter not a
whit. If you're a man, you're wrong; if you're a woman, you're right. ['I
believe her'; 'Believe women'] If you're white, you're privileged (ignore
actual evidence); if you're non-white, you're under-privileged, unless,
of course, you're Asian. Science and logic and argument are all tools
of male oppression. The principles of criminal law, in particular the
principle that those accused of crimes are to be presumed innocent
until proven guilty, are merely devices to prevent rapists being convicted by accusation alone. The old logical fallacy of the *ad hominem* has
now been re-invigorated and elevated to the level of the tribe—it's not
what you say or do, it's which tribe says it or does it.

*E: exalt the new eternal truths and exempt them from questioning or
critical examination*
Western civilisation is inherently racist and sexist and oppressive and
students mustn't be distracted from affirming this article of faith by
anything that might show that the castigated civilisation is actually the
source of the criticism of racism, sexism and oppression. Keep students
away from the classics, ancient or modern, all of them the products of
old white men. On no account are students to read Mill's *On Liberty*
or Locke's *Treatise on Government* or Sophocles's *Antigone* or anything
that might disturb their faith. History is especially *verboten* unless it
serves as a source of examples of just how racist and sexist and oppressive our ancestors were, for which racism, sexism and oppression we
must all atone, even, or especially, those who are not in any way guilty
of those offences. If students read anything at all (and remember,
reading is not all it's cracked up to be) then let them read from the
approved set of orthodox writers who will uncritically reinforce their
insulated set of painfully-acquired prejudices.

Here's a little verse I've composed to encourage you to be an OUTRAGER. Sing it along to the tune of Tammy Wynette's Country & Western classic, D-I-V-O-R-C-E:

Let O-U-T-R-A-G-E
Become total today
Me and my university
Are goin' all the way
I love my chains and it will be
Pure H-E double L for me
If I can't foist this OUTRAGE on
The rest of humanity

Sometimes, I think I've been inadvertently beamed up to a parallel universe! At one time, those who were censored used to be those deemed to be (mostly incorrectly) fascists; now it's anyone whose views are not in line with the current gender/protean sexuality/multicultural/whatever you're having yourself-phobic orthodoxy. Even foundational feminists such as Germaine Greer have come under judgement and been found wanting. Our students have been reared in a cotton-wool culture of comfort, becoming, what Brendan O'Neill calls 'Stepford Students'. Mental and emotional pain of any kind is not, as it is for most people, simply the cost of living in a (relatively) free world, but some kind of radical moral flaw in the universe that must be eliminated at all costs. When I was a student, university authorities censored speech on campus *against* the students' wishes; now, university authorities enforce the banning in accordance with the wishes of the infantilised post 9/11 students who believe that they have a right not to be disturbed, upset or annoyed. They are like children who haven't been allowed to play in the psychic dirt and so haven't developed psychic immunities.

So much for the students. What of the academic staff? Do not, if you value your job as an academic, publish anything that goes against the *zeitgeist*. Bruce Gilley published a paper in 2017 entitled, provocatively, 'The Case for Colonialism'. Cue outrage and calls for the article to be retracted. Almost ten thousand people signed a petition in which they urged the journal's editorial team to 'retract the article and also to apologize for further brutalizing those who have suffered under colonialism.' The petitioners were careful to say that in urging retraction they were not 'curtailing the writer's freedom of speech.' I see. Un-publishing the piece doesn't curtail Gilley's freedom of speech. How silly of me to think just that. The editor-in-chief of the journal claims that the paper was properly subjected to peer review, a claim disputed by some members of the editorial board, fifteen of whom resigned in protest at the publication of the paper. Noam Chomsky, who is also on the journal's editorial board, accepted the contention that proper procedures weren't followed in publishing the article but said, 'I think retraction is a mistake—and also opens very dangerous doors ... Rebuttal offers a great opportunity for education, not only in this case.' It's not often I find myself in agreement with Chomsky but he's right on the money here.

Isn't it standard procedure in cases such as this where it is alleged that, in the words of one critic, Farhana Sultana, what has been published is 'historically inaccurate, lacking in empirical evidence, not engaging with the abundant academic scholarship on the topic, poorly written, conceptually weak, cherry-picks issues/topics, mischaracterizes scholarly work, poor cited and reproduces falsehoods' to rebut the inaccuracies, highlight the lack of empirical evidence, demonstrate the mischaracterisation of scholarly work and spotlight the falsehoods? If the piece is as bad as its critics seem to think it is, shouldn't it be easy to demonstrate this and firmly rebut Gilley's contentions? Apparently not. Why is that? Because, to quote Sultana again, 'Any direct engagement with this piece only amplifies and emboldens horrific ideologies and practices that persist in academia and beyond.' I see. That explains everything.

Much of the criticism by others of Gilley's paper echoed the concerns of Sultana but Nathan J. Robinson went further, comparing Gilley's treatment of Colonialism to Holocaust denial. (Robinson 2017) The idea that defending colonialism is akin to holocaust denial and suggesting that Gilley ignores atrocities committed by colonial powers and by so doing is offensive, makes one wonder why more academics don't find defences of Marxism as a politico-economic theory similarly problematic. But I suppose that is because, as we all know, the atrocities of Marxist regimes were just regrettable anomalies. In 1994, the unrepentant historian Eric Hobsbawm, a lifelong member of the Communist party, felt able to argue that the elimination of millions of people in the Soviet experiment was still justifiable: '[I]n a period in which, as you might say, mass murder and mass suffering are absolutely universal, he said, 'the chance of a new world being born in great suffering would still have been worth backing.' In an interview with Michael Ignatieff in which he made this remark (*Times Literary Supplement* 1994), an incredulous Ignatieff put it to Hobsbawm, 'What that comes down to is saying that had the radiant tomorrow actually been created, the loss of fifteen, twenty million people might have been justified?' to which Hobsbawm replied succinctly and unblushingly, 'Yes.'

Jordan Peterson, the Toronto University professor of psychology, whose public profile went stratospheric when he protested against a Canadian mandatory speech law, received an offer of a Visiting Fellowship from the University of Cambridge, an offer which was subsequently rescinded. The Vice-Chancellor of the University of Cambridge, Stephen Toope, issued a statement on the matter on 25th March 2019 in which he said, 'Early last week, the Faculty [of Divinity] became aware of a photograph of Professor Peterson posing with his arm around a man wearing a T-shirt that clearly bore the slogan "I'm a proud Islamophobe". The *casual endorsement by association* of this message was thought to be antithetical to the work of a Faculty that prides itself in the advancement of inter-faith understanding.' (Emphasis added. See Toope 2019) Casual endorsement by association, eh! While I was an active member of the academic staff in University College Dublin, I associated with all sorts of people—socialists, atheists, radical students—did I thereby casually endorse their views? I suspect that you have associated with a wide variety of people, many of whose views you do not share. By such association, did you therefore casually endorse those views? Toby Young noted that the phrase, 'casual endorsement by association' seemed to be doing the heavy lifting in Cambridge's decision. He went on to say, 'At Peterson's public lectures, a VIP ticket entitles you to be photographed with him and, typically, hundreds are sold. One of the rules is that you're not supposed to stop and chat to Peterson while having your photo taken, because if everyone did the people at the back of the queue would be waiting for hours. So he has only a few seconds with each person—they appear, he puts his arm round them, the photo is taken and then it's on to the next one. Not enough time to scrutinise what's written on their T-shirts, let alone cross-examine them about their political views. So the fact that Peterson was photographed next to this 'proud Islamophobe' does not constitute an 'endorsement' of such views, 'casual' or otherwise.' (Young 2019)

In a delightfully piquant example of the trope, *yes to free speech, but not...*, Professor Toope went on to express his own views on such matters, quoting himself from a previous academic incarnation in which he had said, 'As a university community, we place a paramount value on the free and lawful expression of ideas and viewpoints. As scholars, we believe that discussion across boundaries and across pre-conceptions is a necessary condition for the resolution of even the most intractable conflicts. At the same time, we are a community that values respect for all others, even those with whom we disagree fundamentally. For a university, anything that detracts from the free expression of ideas is just not acceptable. Robust debate can scarcely occur, for example, when some members of the community are made to feel personally attacked, not for their ideas but for their very identity.' (Toope 2019; see also Murray 2019 and Hannan 2019)

Diversity, Inclusion and Equality

'When everyone is somebodee,
Then no one's anybody!'
—W. S. Gilbert

Diversity as a form of intolerance

Some forms of intolerance are egregious and obvious but other forms of intolerance are less blatant and harder to spot. Perhaps chief among the warm-and-fuzzy socially progressive *dogmes de jour* is that of diversity, together with its sister (and effectively interchangeable) dogmas of inclusion and equality, the initial letters of which three pulchritudinally-challenged siblings give us the memorable and entirely appropriate acronym, DIE. Diversity is a special kind of socio-political status accorded to people by virtue of their membership in a group which is deemed to have been historically oppressed or which is currently supposed to be the target of bias or prejudice, a status that allows those people, irrespective of their personal circumstances, to jump to the front of the queue when it comes to the allocation of social goods.

We'll see more of what diversity means shortly but perhaps a preliminary indication of why it is a form of intolerance might be appropriate. In brief, the DIE-versity Dogma consists in a stout refusal to tolerate people's uncoerced choices when the outcomes of those choices clash with the liberal orthodoxy. The DIE-versity Dogmatists manifest a willingness to override the results of those uncoerced choices by legislation or by administrative fiat should such choices, *mirabile dictu,* ever manage to be made. Diversity is a many-headed Hydra but my concern with it in this context is limited to its manifestation as a form of intolerance. (For a superb in-depth treatment of diversity in the round, see Cobley passim.)

For lovers of diversity, diversiphiles, as Peter Wood calls them, diversity is *the* big idea that operates as a sort of power tool to bring about the secular eschaton. 'Diversity,' writes Wood, 'sees itself as a tool for knocking down the door to exclusive enclaves—colleges, workplaces churches, organizations of all sorts—of the favored groups.' (Wood 2003, 5) On the other hand, there are those casuistical cynics, such as myself, who see diversity simply as a strategy for implementing and instituting new and more imaginative forms of discrimination and privilege, a form of affirmative action for the twenty-teens or, as Wood puts it, a 'rubric for racial and ethnic quotas in college admissions and on the job; for acts of petty and not so petty discrimination; and for a system of ethnic favoritism that undercuts the principle of rewarding demonstrated merit and ability. *Diversity*, to its critics, calls to mind cultural elites who promulgate convoluted reasons why discrimination is wrong, except when they do it.' (Wood 2003, 6)

In its dictionary meaning, *diversity* simply connotes the condition or quality of being different. For a Liberal Newspeaker, however, *diversity* is a term that applies to people who differ from one another by virtue of their membership of particular groups, groups characterised by race, religion, sex and sexual preference, which groups have ostensibly been denied privileges that have been enjoyed by others. Diversiphiles hold as an article of faith that membership in a victimised group entitles one to special privileges. In the case of previously discriminated-against groups, their current successors are entitled to compensation because of the previous prejudicial treatment of their ancestors and the supposed continuing disadvantage that members of such groups experience. Diversity, Woods writes, 'is about treating groups as having saved up a right to special privileges in proportion to how much their purported ancestors were victimized in the past.' (Wood 2003, 10) It may not be immediately obvious just what is so special or wonderful about diversity that invests it with such transcendent moral significance; after all, everyone is diverse from everybody else in some way or another. But some people, it seems are more diverse than others. In the special sense that the term *diversity* has acquired, pretty much everyone is diverse in some significant respect or other, unless that person happens to be white, male, Christian, conservative or heterosexual.

Diversity, then, is to be understood to apply to race (if it exists), sex (if there is any such thing), gender (if it is different from sex or even, perhaps especially, if it isn't), age, religion, sexual preference, ethnicity, language, and political beliefs of the right (sorry left) sort. This list is not closed and other categories may be added as the spirit of the age moves. Diversity, however, most emphatically does *not* apply to certain modes of thinking, especially those conservative modes of thought that would call the sacred DIE-versity Dogma itself into question. Conservative presumptions and conservative conclusions are not forms of thought that enjoy the protection of diversity. According to the dictionary, a *conservative* is an adherent of traditional values, ideas, and institutions, an opponent of social and political change but, of course, every speaker of Liberal Newspeak knows that *conservative* is a general term of abuse to be applied to anyone of whom she disapproves. Ideological diversity is not a *desideratum*. To the best of my knowledge, no university or Googleoid corporation is trying desperately to hire conservatives. If your social group has been assimilated, it cannot be diverse. Diversity is a status that, once lost, is lost forever. Italian-Americans or German-Americans or Polish-Americans can be poor or face prejudice but if they try to identify with their ethnic heritages so as to don the mantle of diversity they are in for a rude shock. Similarly, if your social group is successful, it is in great danger of losing its claim to any diverse status. It is never acceptable to wonder why certain minority groups match and even exceed so-called representational norms, despite having suffered prejudice and oppression in the past. Asian-Americans are sometimes said to be over-represented in premier universities. As it happens, Asian-Americans are not overrepresented at premier campuses any more than other groups are underrepresented. The notion of representation simply has no application here. What we have here are just individuals making individual decisions having individual histories and individual academic successes, not tokens of a type or representatives of a kind. But this is to anticipate our discussion on representation. (see § 'Diversity, equality and representation' below)

The notion that group identity trumps individuality is central to the idea of diversity. Diversity is based on the idea that people should properly be seen in relation to each other primarily as members of racial and ethnic groups and any other group deemed to be diverse-relevant and *not* as individuals who have equal rights before the law. One of the glories of Western civilisation has been the emergence of and celebration of the individual human being in all his individuality and not merely as a token or representative of any class or religion or race. If we now turn our backs on this singular cultural achievement and start to deal with people not as individuals but as the intersection of the various classes that they supposedly 'represent', then we are well on the way to reverting to a form of tribalism.

Of course, all the identitarian nonsense is just the latest example of collectivism at work. According to the collectivist dogma, I am who I am because of what I am and what I am is given to me by the collectivity I belong to that is most in favour today. Yesterday it was class—I was a proletarian, a bourgeois, a capitalist; today it is race or ethnicity. But whatever the givens of our lives—where we were born, who our parents are, what language or languages we natively speak, none of which we chose—all this is the basic material which constrains our lives without determining them. The glory of being human is that who we are transcends all our contingent givens. The history of the human race has been a long and sometimes sad story of our emergence as individuals from group identities; identity politics turns us around and points us back in the wrong direction. (see Casey 2017, 22-7)

For many of the Left today, anyone who speaks in favour of group blindness is on the wrong side of history. For some, especially those on college campuses, anyone who doesn't swallow the anti-oppression orthodoxy hook, line, and sinker, anyone who doesn't acknowledge 'white supremacy' in America, is a racist. To suggest that one should be indifferent to group identity today is to invite accusations of collusion in oppression. Even that icon of the left, 2016 would-be US presidential candidate Bernie Sanders, got into trouble when he suggested that it wasn't enough for someone to say 'Hey, I'm Latina, vote for me!'

White privilege?

If prizes are to be had in the oppression stakes, then it was only a matter of time before men and white people (and the inevitable fatal combination, white men) entered the race. Even people who think of themselves as moderate but are daily maligned because of their maleness or whiteness and the privilege that is supposed to be associated with all that feel the urge to push back. Not every white man is high in the social pecking order. Those who aren't, and they are many, ask themselves why they are being attacked and they are inclined to group together with others for what they see as self-defence.

For quite some time, slowly but, it seemed, inexorably, race or ethnicity was moving in the direction of 'Yes....but so what'. Yes, I'm white, but so what. Yes, I'm black, but so what. Race and ethnicity was beginning to have about as much intrinsic connection to what one is at the core of one's being as one's height or weight but identity politics has stalled or perhaps even reversed the progress we were making in that direction. All forms of identitarian politics are ridiculous, white, black or any other shade on the colour spectrum but somehow, only assertions of white identity are routinely jeered at and patronised and regarded as ridiculous. But what is sauce for the goose is sauce for the gander and either all forms of racial or ethnic identitarianism are justifiable or none is. One effect, one undoubtedly unintended effect, of victimoid identity politics is to make white identity something that becomes politically significant. It has violated one of the basic rules of the Harry Potter world; *draco dormiens nunquam titillandus*—never tickle a sleeping dragon or, to change literary references, it has woken the Kraken.

But isn't it the case that to be white is to be the beneficiary of immense privilege? Ah yes, white privilege, a packet of benefits that supposedly accrues to every white person simply by virtue of their being white. When it comes to actually delineating these supposed privileges, however, examples are thin on the ground. White privilege is to racism what the patriarchy is to feminism, a mythical if somewhat fugitive beast that supposedly represses and suffocates non-whites. The meaning of the word 'privilege' is that of a law made specifically for the benefit of one person or group of people to the detriment of others. White privilege, then, strictly speaking means laws that specifically benefit white people and only white people. I am not aware of the existence of any such laws. On the contrary, in the USA and also, to some degree in the UK, if there are any laws that privilege one racial or ethnic group over another, these laws privilege non-whites over whites. Perhaps we should be talking about non-white privilege?

What, if it's not rude to ask, is the evidence for white privilege? Well, on the educational front, it turns out in the UK that black, minority and ethnic students (BMEs) are more likely to be excluded from school than non-BMEs, less likely to achieve entry to a Russell University than non-BMEs. Those BMEs who do enter university are more likely to drop out and less likely to achieve a First or 2/1 than non-BMEs. BMEs when employed tend to earn less than non-BMEs and to have a greater rate of unemployment. Few of the top jobs in the UK go to BMEs, even in education.

Well, this is not good but what does it tell us? By itself, nothing. If these are facts, they are facts. The disparities may be the result of some kind of actual discrimination, some illegitimate use of force or law to depress the ambitions of BMEs. On the other hand, the disparities may be the resultant of other factors. Before a claim of discrimination can be sustained, we need evidence to support that claim and that evidence cannot be the mere fact of the disparities.

The prospect of people claiming some kind of white identity that entitles them to special privileges is more than faintly absurd. I did not choose to be white; my whiteness was thrust upon me. Being white doesn't accord me any particular merit or demerit and neither should it. I don't feel proud of being white nor do I feel ashamed. Either of these two emotional attitudes to my being white is completely futile. With the emergence of identity politics, however, and the idea that the possession of a particular skin colour or membership of a particular ethnic group connotes some kind of special virtue, the knock-on effect is for all people to begin to do the same, including whites. It now seems that well over half of all Americans consider their being white important to their identity!

It is more than a little ironic that at the very time when, apart from a few irredeemable recidivists, the idea of the superiority of the white race has more or less fallen into oblivion, critical race theory and its companions have emerged to suggest that white people are in their heart of hearts, racist to the core, whether consciously or unconsciously, intentionally or unintentionally. If the evidence for conscious white racism is hard to come by, then most white racism must be unconscious. The trouble with this, as with the notion of unconscious bias in general, is that it becomes a kind of original sin from which no white person is exempt and of which every white person is guilty regardless of whether or not there is any actual evidence for or manifestation of this supposed sense of racial superiority. The trouble with the concept of unconscious racism as with the postulation of all unconscious attributes is that it's irrefutable in principle. Loudly proclaiming that one is not racist, if one is white, is simply taken to be a typical defensive strategy serving to conceal the very racism that is being denied! A refusal to confess and repent of one's white privilege is yet another piece of evidence to support the claim of implicit or unconscious white racism.

Diversity, equality and representation

Diversity employs a bizarre and empirically vacuous notion of representation based on the idea that particular groups should be represented in the allocation of high-status jobs and other social goods in a manner that matches the groups' relative proportions in the general population. For diversiphiles, equality is to be understood in numerically proportional terms, not in terms of the boring bourgeois notion of the equal standing of individuals before the law. 'Real equality,' writes Wood, 'according to the diversicrats, consists of parity among groups, and to achieve it, social goods must be measured out in ethnic quotas, purveyed by group preferences, or otherwise filtered according to the will of social factions.' (Wood 2003, 14) Social benefits, especially high-paying and important jobs but also, for example, admission to prestigious universities, are to be distributed according to the proportion of any relevant group in the general population unless such groups have previously been, or are currently deemed to be, discriminated against, in which case they may (and should) enjoy a *greater* share of social benefits than their numbers would otherwise warrant! There is no requirement, however, that low-paying, unpleasant or dangerous jobs be proportionately distributed. If one were to be cynical once more, one might think that this kind of equality is really inequality but inequality of the right (that is, left) kind.

Actions, policies, procedures and laws that disadvantage members of groups that are deemed to have been guilty of any form of oppression in the past or are currently deemed to be engaged in oppression are perfectly in order, irrespective of the actual guilt or innocence of individual members of such groups. The guilt of such groups (and the individuals within such groups) is to be determined exclusively by members in good standing of groups putatively previously disadvantaged. No appeal is possible against this determination of guilt and efforts by those accused to demonstrate their innocence will be taken as *prima facie* evidence of guilt or of continuing oppression. Where those groups who are deemed to have been discriminated against historically or currently (pretty much everybody except straight white men, according to the diversity gospel) enjoy a *greater* proportion of social benefits than their numbers in the general population would warrant, this is *not* to be presumed as violating the principle of non-discrimination but as simply being part of the natural order of things or as constituting the partial rectification of past wrongs.

The seemingly innocent term *representation* as used by diversiphiles conceals a problem at its heart, like a worm i' the bud. I was employed by University College Dublin for almost thirty years. While I was thus employed, I didn't represent Corkmen, males, the elderly, white people, keen but mediocre chess players, ardent classical music lovers, people over 5' 11", the constitutionally cranky or anyone else. It wasn't that I failed to represent them or that I represented others; I simply wasn't in the business of representation at all! Similarly, if a woman is employed by the Acme Explosives Company, she doesn't thereby represent women any more than a disabled person employed by Hibernian Hirsute Industries represents the disabled. In general, any person manifesting characteristic X does not by that fact represent Xs.

Our diversiphiles might respond, 'This is just a verbal quibble. What we're concerned about is not any notion of representation as agency or delegation but something different and much more important, namely, the proportion of Xs and Ys and Zs to be found in all sectors of society and how well or otherwise these proportions match the proportions of Xs, Ys and Zs in the population as a whole.' Well, alright. Point taken. But why call it representation then? Confucius is reputed to have said that if he ever became a government minister, his first task would be to ensure the rectification of names. Calling things by the right names isn't the solution to all our problems but calling them by the wrong names is certain to obstruct the attainment of our goals. Let's take it, then, that what our diversiphiles are talking about as representation is actually some kind of relative proportionality and let's examine *that* notion. At the heart of the diversiphile's position lies the assumption that, absent human malignity, the proportion of Xs, Ys and Zs in private or government employment or in acting or in music or in any kind of trade, activity or profession would mirror the proportion of Xs, Ys and Zs in the general population. But this is an assumption and, moreover, it is one that flies in the face of both experience and logic. Thomas Sowell makes this point and does so with his customary exemplary clarity.

> Neither in nature nor among human beings are either equal or randomly distributed outcomes automatic. On the contrary, grossly unequal distributions of outcomes are common, both in nature and among people, in circumstances where neither genes nor discrimination are involved....The idea that [the world] would be a level playing field, if it were not for either genes or discrimination, is a preconception in defiance of both logic and facts. Nothing is easier to find than sins among human beings, but to automatically make those sins the sole, or even primary, cause of different outcomes among different peoples is to ignore many other reasons for those disparities. (Sowell 2018, 18)

> At the heart of many discussions of disparities among individuals, groups and nations is the seemingly invincible fallacy that outcomes in human endeavors would be equal, or at least comparable or

random, if there were no biased interventions, on the one hand, nor genetic deficiencies, on the other. This preconception, which spans the ideological spectrum is in utter defiance of both logic and empirical evidence from around the world, and over millennia of recorded history .... Nor is discrimination automatically excluded. It is one of many possibilities, each of which has to establish its claims with evidence rather than being an automatic presumption. (Sowell 2018, 100-101)

Speaking at an event in March 2019, Lady Hale, president of the UK's Supreme Court, who is Britain's most senior judge, called for at least half of the judiciary to be made up of women. Her reason for this manifesto is that since women make up half the population, they should be half the judges at least. Lady Hale's idiosyncratic ideology is not confined to mathematical prescriptivism. Previously, she advocated more diversity in the judiciary so that 'the public feel those on the bench are "our judges" rather than "beings from another planet". It must be a great consolation when you are being sent down for a 15-year stretch to have your sentence handed out by someone of the same sex and race as yourself. I presume that by parity of reasoning, Lady Hale would recommend that women should also make up half of the roof workers, garbage collectors and oil rig workers and, since men make up half the population, *they* should make up half of nurses, secretaries and teachers. Forced job swaps would rapidly create equality between the sexes. We should insist that 'bin men' swap with primary school teachers; building workers with nurses and car thieves with social workers. Diversity-as-equality, which is really jobs for the girls and other victim-privileged groups, is always sought in the more glamorous areas of employment: TV, entertainment, politics, the higher levels of business administration, never on road-repair crews or down coal mines. In the end, it's not equality for women but equality (read = special privileges) for *women-like-me*.

Male executives at Britain's biggest companies must lead the charge by bringing more women into senior positions, the 2019 British Home Secretary and Women and Equalities Minister Amber Rudd, said, as she urged companies to embrace 50/50 gender shortlists. Leaving aside the not-insignificant fact that there are now many more than two genders, the Home Secretary didn't say why companies should do this so I presume the reason for it is supposed to be obvious. But it's not obvious to me.

Here's a simple question. Why 50/50 gender (whatever *that* is) representation? Why not 52.7%/47.3% representation? And why for gender, so-called (really for sex, since there are very many genders but only two sexes)? Why not for race? (Is there any such thing as race? And if so, how many races are there?) Why not for disability? age? height? hair colour? shoe size? or just about any other difference you might choose to select? Why the presumption that anything less than 50/50 is somehow a bad thing, almost certainly the result of some kind of dastardly discrimination.

It might prove difficult to get the proportions right once all relevant groups are taken into consideration. The UK Construction Week banned the use by exhibitors of attractive scantily clothed females to help sell their products. The organisers told the exhibitors, 'Consider the mix of staff you have on the stand (gender, age, ethnicity etc.). Do they represent the diversity of your company? And if not, be prepared to explain why not.' Explain what and to whom and why? And what's all this about the diversity of your company? Let's think about this for a little while. One commentator wrote, if you're going to take diversity seriously and not just tokenise it, 'To accurately represent the racial diversity of say, England and Wales, on every stand you would have to have 102 Whites, 2 Mixed Race, 7 Asians, 3 Blacks, 1 Chinese.' But, as he points out, things quickly get a little more complex when you 'start accounting for gender identity and sexuality and ignoring any diversity along other lines of heritage (Indian/Pakistani, African/West Indian etc.).' It's getting complicated. But wait, there's more. 'To get a gay person of Chinese extraction into the mix you'll need to hire 18 Chinese (1 gay), and over 2200 white people (120+ gay).' It's getting even more complicated. 'But of course you'd have to do the same for the "Trans Community". GIRES touts a population of 300,000 trans people out of a general population of 65m, so you'd need to hire e.g. 25,000 white people (1450 gays) to ensure you get your transgendered Chinese person (200+ Chinese in total, of which 12 gay).'

Terry Gilliam of Monty Python fame had his say on diversity in response to the BBC's Controller of Comedy Commissioning who said 'If you're going to assemble a team now, it's not going to be six Oxbridge white blokes. It's going to be a diverse range of people who reflect the modern world.' Gilliam's response can be summed up in one word—bullshit! 'Now we need one of this, one of that, everybody represented ... this is bullshit. I no longer want to be a white male, I don't want to be blamed for everything wrong in the world: I tell the world now I'm a black lesbian... My name is Loretta and I'm a BLT, a black lesbian in transition.' Well, why not? If we can identify ourselves as anything we choose, why can't Gilliam choose to identify as a BLT. Thus identified, he will all by himself be the acme of diversity.

We can glean some idea of why diversity is desirable from the pronouncements of Jayne-Anne Gadhia, the Government's Women and Finance champion. She tells us that 'A balanced workforce is good for staff, customers, productivity and profitability.' Really? How interesting! I wonder how she knows this? Would it be possible to see some, ahem, evidence to support this claim, or is it supposed to be true *a priori*?

One way to achieve diversity between the sexes is by the use of quotas. On this topic, Elizabeth Wasserman writing in the *National Post* in 2015 says it for me when she writes, 'the very idea of gender quotas turns my stomach.' Her reason for this apparently unsisterly judgement is that, 'I'm against gender quotas and browbeating campaigns, not just because they impose unnecessary burdens on private enterprise and represent an overly simplistic view of "diversity," but because I believe the coerced promotion of females would represent two steps back on the road to equality.' She goes on to make what I believe to be an irrefutable point.

> The worst thing women can do for ourselves in the workplace is to make ourselves objects of fear and suspicion, making it politically impossible to fire us or to pass us over for promotion, requiring male colleagues to walk on eggshells and to wonder whether our hiring was

politically motivated, and forcing us to wonder the same. Women are a majority in universities and in the workforce; we are nearly 50% of medical and law students. We may be underrepresented in the fields of technology or business, but that's a matter of choice. At a certain point, when we demand an equal ratio of men to women in certain fields, what we're criticizing is not 'the system,' but the choices that women themselves are making.

What can I say, Ms Wasserman, except to give your trenchant observation my whole-hearted assent. Of course, the false consciousness feminists will tell us that women don't really know what's good for them (women other than themselves, of course) so their choices don't have to be respected!

And what of that perennial paroxysm of petulance, the so-called gender pay gap? Two studies provide strong evidence that the so-called pay gap between men and women has little to do with gender discrimination and almost everything to do with women being free to discriminate (that is, freely decide) how they spend their time. Shock! Horror! Surely that can't be true! The first study dealing with a gender earnings gap in the gig economy based itself on information drawn from over a million rideshares. It found that there was approximately a 7% gap between male and female drivers. Discrimination? Well, hardly, since all employment decisions are made by the drivers themselves. Among the factors relevant to explaining the earnings difference, the authors of the study suggest preferences relating to where and when to work and, surprisingly, preferences for driving speed. (see Cook et al.) The second study found that in 67 countries or regions, girls on average do as well on science tests as boys, and women would do as well as men in university-level mathematics and science courses—if they were prepared to actually take them! However, the paper also shows that in countries in which girls have *greater* choice and face *less* discrimination, there are fewer women in science, technology, engineering and technology (STEM)! The authors of the study call this, with good reason, the educational-gender-equality paradox. (see Stoet and Geary] 'One of the main findings of this study is that, paradoxically, countries with lower levels of gender equality had relatively more women among STEM graduates than did more gender-equal countries. This is a paradox, because gender-equal countries are those that give girls and women more educational and empowerment opportunities and that generally promote girls' and women's engagement in STEM fields.'

In their explanation of the paradox, the authors speculate that it appears to be connected with choice. While the average girl is as good at science as the average boy, she is even stronger in reading. In countries in which women have more choice, as well as greater financial security, they are more likely to choose careers that provide lower financial rewards but greater quality of life, or, as the authors of the study put it, 'One possibility is that the liberal mores in these cultures, combined with smaller financial costs of foregoing a STEM path ... amplify the influence of intra-individual academic strengths. The result would be the differentiation of the academic foci of girls and boys during secondary education and later in college, and across time, increasing sex differences in science as an academic strength and in graduation with STEM degrees.'

So, if what we want is numerically equal representation of women in STEM subjects, it seems that we should give women *fewer choices* and *increase their financial insecurity*. Or—and I know this may sound mad—perhaps, we should simply give up the futile and absurd idea that numerical equality of men and women in any field is a consummation devoutly to be wished and admit that a truly equitable society would be one in which individuals (not groups) were free to make their own choices for their own reasons.

Occasionally there's a glimmer of humour among all this grim nonsense. It seems that Oxford is to put an end to its women-only fellowships because they breach equality laws! One such fellowship is the Joanna Randall-MacIver Fellowship which was set up in the 1930s for women to help them to study fine arts, music or literature. One previous recipient of this fellowship, Professor Alexandra Wilson, said 'I do think it's a rather regrettable consequence of a well-intended law that this opportunity for women should be removed.' (Turner 2019) My heart bleeds for you, Professor Wilson, it really does.

James Damore, anyone?

Remember James Damore? He was the software engineer who was summarily fired from Google for daring to suggest that their policy on diversity wasn't all that it was cracked up to be. He wrote a memo entitled 'Google's Ideological Echo Chamber: How Bias Clouds Our Thinking About Diversity and Inclusion' in which he suggested, among other things, that there might be some factors other than outright discrimination to account for the different proportions of men and women in IT, such as a different distribution of traits between men and women, and (and this is probably where he committed the unforgiveable sin) that positive discrimination to reach an equal representation of men and women is unfair, divisive and actually bad for business.

Damore had the cheek, nay the temerity, to suggest that the significantly larger number of men than women in tech fields might have something to do with individual choice and something to do with some innate differences between men and women. His first suggestion ran clean against the progressive dogma which is that all disparities in ratios between significant groups (in this case, men and women) are *always* due to discrimination, overt or covert. His second suggestion violated one of the new 10 commandments—'There are no differences of any kind between men and women. If anyone asserts the contrary, let him be anathema; p.s. disregard all empirical evidence.'

The memo created an online storm and, in a singular demonstration of their commitment to diversity, Google fired Damore in August 2017. According to Google's Vice-President for Diversity, Danielle Brown, 'Part of building an open, inclusive environment means fostering a culture in which those with alternative views, including different political views, feel safe sharing their opinions. But that discourse needs to work alongside the principles of equal employment found in our Code of Conduct, policies, and anti-discrimination laws'. Supporting Browne's statement, Google's CEO, Sundar Pichai, wrote 'to suggest a group of our colleagues have traits that make them less biologically suited to that work is offensive and not OK ... At the same time, there are co-workers who are questioning whether they can safely express their views in the workplace (especially those with a minority viewpoint). They too feel under threat, and that is also not OK.' Put the Browne and Pichai statements together and you get a HenryFordish 'any colour you like so long as its black' statement of ideological diversity—as a Google employee you can share your alternative views and feel safe in so doing, provided that those views don't blaspheme against the sacred doctrines of diversity.

You may be glad to learn that Damore is fighting back. He has initiated a suit against Google alleging systematic bias: racial bias against whites, gender bias against men, and political bias against conservatives. Damore's complaint runs to a mere 181 pages and is astonishing for the anti-white, anti-male and anti-conservative culture is reveals. Of particular interest are the screen shots of internal Google communications and posts on message boards that seem to suggest *prima facie* evidence of an environment hostile to white men. The online reactions to Damore's memo tend to validate his analysis of the authoritarian and repressive atmosphere in Google, consisting as they do for the most part of the usual slurs of racist, sexist, homophobe and bigot.

Commenting on the Damore memo, Professor Lee Jussim of Rutgers University remarks that the memo 'gets nearly all of the science and its implications exactly right. Its main points are that: 1. Neither the left nor the right gets diversity completely right; 2. The social science evidence on implicit and explicit bias has been wildly oversold and is far weaker than most people seem to realize; 3. Google has, perhaps unintentionally, created an authoritarian atmosphere that has stifled discussion of these issues by stigmatizing anyone who disagrees as a bigot and instituted authoritarian policies of reverse discrimination; 4. The policies and atmosphere systematically ignore biological, cognitive, educational, and social science research on the nature and sources of individual and group differences.' (Jussim 2017)

Professor Geoffrey Miller of the University of New Mexico says, 'I think that almost all of the Google memo's empirical claims are scientifically accurate. Moreover, they are stated quite carefully and dispassionately. Its key claims about sex differences are especially well-supported by large volumes of research across species, cultures, and history.' Miller notes that 'Blank slate gender feminism is advocacy rather than science: no gender feminist I've met has ever been able to give a coherent answer to the question "What empirical findings would convince you that psychological sex differences evolved?"' (see Anon. 2017c) He makes a point relevant to the feminist gender theory two step commonly danced around the notions of equality and diversity. The standard dogma contains two premises: 1. The human sexes and races have exactly the same minds, attitudes and dispositions, and 2. The human sexes and races have radically different minds, attitudes and dispositions. There is a pretty obvious contradiction between 1. and 2. If you adhere to 1, you'll believe that outcome inequalities between sexes and races are due to systemic racism and sexism; If you adhere to 2, you'll believe that outcome inequalities are not (necessarily) due to systemic racism and sexism.

The usual argument for gender diversity is that a gender-balanced corporate management will prevent it from being dominated exclusively by either male or female thinking. But, of course, if there's no essential difference between male and female thinking in the first place, then it wouldn't matter whether your corporate team was 100% female or 100% male or anything else in between and then your rationale for gender diversity flies out the window. The same goes for racial diversity. So, as Professor Miller puts it, 'if the sexes and races don't differ at all, and if psychological interchangeability is true, then there's no practical business case for diversity.' But if diversity is to be justifiable, it must be because there *are* important differences in how the minds of different genders (sexes) and races work. The trouble with this of course is that if such differences exist, then they are pertinent to the kind of skills and competencies and motivations that are relevant to employment and promotion. Professor Miller again, 'if demographic diversity yields any competitive advantages due to psychological differences between groups, then demographic equality of outcome cannot be achieved in all jobs and all levels within a company. At least, not without discriminatory practices such as affirmative action or demographic quotas.'

Let's go over this important point one more time. Here are two contrary propositions. 1. males and females have exactly the same minds with exactly the same aptitudes, motivations, interests, competencies, traits and so on, so that if there is any inequality in hiring (as measured against the ratios of male/females in general population) this can be due only to discrimination. (Ditto for different races). 2. males and females have radically different minds with different aptitudes, motivations, interests, competencies, traits so that companies should hire diversely in order to increase their reservoir of skills and talents. If, on this assumption, we don't have diversity, this represents a management failure.

Of course, 1 and 2 can't both be true! If 1 is true, then there is no particular reason to promote diversity in your company. A and B and C are all interchangeable and it makes no difference what sex or race A, B and C are. Diversity cannot lend a company any competitive advantage and so there is no business case to be made for it. However, if 2 is true, then diversity *can* give a company a competitive advantage. But, if minds and their characteristics vary significantly across sex and race, then it is unlikely that a company is going to have some ratio of male/female, race 1/race2/ race 3, etc. that reflects the ratios of those sexes and races in the general population, unless, of course, the coercive power of the law is used to bring this about. In short: if we start with psychological fungibility, diversity becomes pointless; if we start with psychological unfungibility, then equality is not guaranteed. Which do you want to have? Equality or diversity.

Inclusion

We must not only be diverse, we must also be inclusive. One place where inclusivity has become a *cause célèbre* is in the acting profession, that realm of rogues and vagabonds. Here, inclusivity takes the form of what is called 'authenticity casting'. Bryan Cranston, the star of *Breaking Bad*, was criticised for playing the part of a quadriplegic billionaire in the 2017 film, *The Upside*. Why? Because

Cranston isn't quadriplegic! Oddly enough, nobody criticised him for playing the part of a billionaire when he's not a billionaire. Cranston, to his eternal credit, has refused to bow down to the demands of the *biens pensants* and has vigorously defended his playing of the part. In a similar way, the actor Simon Callow, speaking of his role, or rather 37 roles, in his one-man *A Christmas Carol*, remarked sarcastically, 'I am neither fat, young, female, or paraplegic ... but have been labouring under the misapprehension that the audience was enjoying my capacity for transformation.'

In another delightfully insane plot twist, proponents of authenticity casting assert that it is no longer appropriate for actors to attempt accents that are not their own; to do so is to commit the sin of cultural appropriation. I thought, and you probably thought likewise, that actors were people who made a living out of pretending to be what they are not. It's true, of course, that some actors' attempts at accents are shockingly bad but the problem with that is not their attempting those accents, it's doing them very badly! In a *Guardian* piece (March 2019), Vanessa Thorpe writes, 'When Scottish film star Sean Connery delivered his lines in the 1987 hit *The Untouchables* in a ripe Irish brogue, not all the cinema audience was convinced. Yet his right to have a go at a different accent was not questioned.' True on both counts, Ms Thorpe. The accent was shockingly bad but why shouldn't he have a go? She continues, 'If it happened today, however, Connery might feel the need to make it clear from the get-go that his paternal grandparents were of Irish descent.' Well, who cares? Irish grandparents or no Irish grandparents, Connery's attempt at an Irish accent in *The Untouchables* is still rotten! Which would you prefer—an actor without Irish ancestry who can deliver an authentic or at least what sounds like an authentic Irish accent or an actor like Sean Connery, with genuine Irish ancestry, who sounds as if he were just about to say, 'Sure and begorrah, here's the old news, bejapers!' I know which one I'd prefer. In Neil Jordan's *Michael Collins*, we have examples of the best and the worst of Irish accents. Julia Roberts, in her character of Kitty Kiernan, seems to have taken Sean Connery's correspondence course while the late Alan Rickman, who to the best of my knowledge didn't have a drop of Irish blood in him, delivered an eerily accurate version of what would have seemed to most Irish people to be simply inimitable, the idiosyncratic vocal strains of Éamon de Valera. The film as a whole was an historical travesty, of course, but Rickman was one of the few actors who came away from it with any credit. But, as Thorpe notes, it is no longer a matter of whether you do a good or a bad job of acting. Now, as she puts it, 'An actor's automatic licence to fake an accent is now increasingly in doubt. Casting agents are under growing pressure to find talent that matches the background of a character if they want to avoid accusations of cultural appropriation, or even, in some cases, the charge of outright mockery.'

What authenticity casting comes right down to is that it is no longer enough for actors to fake accents or characters or, to put it another way, it is not enough for them to act. They must now genuinely possess the nationality, the accent, and the other aspects of the characters they are playing. According to the diktats of authenticity casting, only disabled actors can portray characters who are disabled—so goodbye to Daniel Day-Lewis and his moving portrayal of Christy Brown in *My Left Foot*. Only mentally challenged actors can portray mentally challenged characters— so goodbye to Dustin Hoffman in *Rainman*. Will we reach a stage in which only murderers will be permitted to portray murderers, sadists sadists, and child molesters child molesters? If not, why not? Why shouldn't we demand the full Monty when it comes to authenticity? At the root of the authenticity casting mania lies what we might call the general representational principle (GRP): Only actors who *are* X can *play* X. This principle, if applied consistently, is going to put a lot of actors out of work. I know that actors say hyperbolically that they would murder for a part but I'm not sure just how many of them are fully committed to carrying this promise through!

There is a point, a small point, to this representational nonsense, which is that it may sometimes make sense, from a casting perspective to select actors who display some of the characteristics of the characters they portray. Other things being equal, it would seem

sensible to cast women in female roles and men in male roles—
obvious exceptions would include films of the *Victor Victoria* or
Shakespeare in Love genre—but in the end, acting is pretence and
what matters is the ability of the actors chosen for a role, whatever
their actual characteristics, to persuade an audience by the exercise
of the dark arts of acting that they are what they pretend to be. I
am reminded of the story that is told (and it is too good not to be
true) of the conversation that took place between Dustin Hoffman
and Laurence Olivier while they were making *Marathon Man*.
Hoffman's character was supposed not to have slept for 72 hours
so, as befits a method actor, Hoffman claimed that he hadn't slept
for 72 hours in order to achieve a kind of Stanilavskyian degree of
verisimilitude. Olivier was bemused and is reported to have said,
'My dear boy, why don't you just try acting?'

Happily, not all actors are persuaded of the transparent truth
of the GRP. Thorpe quotes the actor Simon Callow as saying,
'Nobody who has talent should be kept out of the acting
profession. And nobody, even white, middle-class males, should
be prevented from playing any part.' In much the same vein, Sheila
Hancock, the daughter of a publican, remarked that in an environment in which characters could only play versions of themselves,
'I'd be bored stiff. When I started, I was deemed only able to play
maids.' Now she is allowed more range. 'I've played northern recently, too, as well as someone with dementia—and I certainly don't
have that.'

Scarlett Johansson was attacked on the basis of the GRP when it
was reported that she was going to play a trans man in an upcoming
movie based on real life events. Some critics said that since the
character she was intending to play, Jean Marie Gill or Dante 'Tex'
Gill was a trans man who went by a male name, her insistence on
playing the part misrepresented the details of his story. Ah yes, of
course. For true verisimilitude, the part requires to be played by an
actor who *is* a trans man. Another complainant claimed that having
Johansson play the part would perpetuate the notion that transgender people are just playing dress up with their gender. Really? Why
ever would we think that?

What authenticity casting comes down to in the end, however, is jobs for the boys or girls or people who are neither boys or girls. It's been pointed out, with what degree of accuracy I don't know, that whereas cisgendered actors (actors who aren't suffering from the delusion that they're not the sex that they are) can play trans roles and non-trans roles, trans actors are limited to playing trans characters so that when Johansson takes the role she's been castigated for taking, she deprives some unfortunate trans actor of a job.

Sierra Boggess, the woman who was to have sung the role of Maria in *West Side Story* at the BBC Proms, relinquished her position in April 2018 after complaints were made that casting a 'non-Latina face' (whatever *that* is) in the role was an example of 'whitewashing'. Apparently feeling the force of these complaints, Boggess said that she had come to realise that if she were to persist in the role, it 'would once again deny Latinas the opportunity to sing this score, as well as deny the importance of seeing themselves represented on stage.' Yes, Ms Boggess, it's really important to see people of our kind (whatever *that* is) represented on the stage; otherwise, our self-esteem is likely to take a severe knock. In any event, Ms Boggess has learnt her lesson well and is duly repentant. BBC News reports her as saying, 'Since the announcement of this concert, I have had many conversations about why this is a crucial time, now more than ever, to not perpetuate the miscasting of this show. I apologise for not coming to this realisation sooner and as an artist, I must ask myself how I can best serve the world, and in this case my choice is clearer than ever: to step aside and allow an opportunity to correct a wrong that has been done for years with this show in particular. I have therefore withdrawn myself from this concert and I look forward to continuing to be a voice for change in our community and our world!' I am sure we all wish Ms Boggess the best of luck in her desire to serve the world, a world which is, no doubt, eagerly awaiting her service.

Ms Boggess has been replaced by a singer who is described as being of 'mixed heritage' so I suppose that half rights the grievous wrong that has been done hitherto. Perhaps it's worth pointing out that in the Bernstein-directed studio recording of *West Side Story*, the part of Tony was sung by José Carreras whose singing was wonderful but whose pronunciation when singing sounded very much like the way speakers of Spanish speak English, which is ever so slightly problematic in the context of *West Side Story* given that Tony is supposed to be a member of the non-Spanish speaking gang! Now *that* was a spectacular bit of miscasting if ever there was one!

Staying in the land of the luvvies for a moment, it's good to know that it doesn't matter if the reason your movie was a flop was because it was a terrible movie if you can blame its failure on lack of diversity. Guy Richie's *King Arthur: Legend of the Sword* was a massive flop but if only it had had more women in it everything would have been all right. Yeah, sure. A male turkey is always a turkey but a female turkey is sometimes a swan. Movies are good if they make politically correct statements either in their content or in their casting. Forget entertainment, direction, script, cinematography and all the rest. Just have it be about the right issues, take the right angle on those issues, have a suitably diverse cast and crew and, above all, do not have it commit any of the NO-NOs—no racism (explicit or implicit), no misogyny (explicit or implicit), no heteronormativity (explicit or implicit), *ad infinitum*.

BBC World reported that Hollywood was criticised for a drop in the number of LGBT characters that appeared in its films in 2017. (BBC News 2018) Which leads me to ask, is there some specific percentage of LGBT characters that should be portrayed in films and, if so, what is that percentage and how do we know what that percentage is? The Gay and Lesbian Alliance Against Defamation which has the Pollyanna-ish acronym GLAAD found that 12% of mainstream releases featured LGBT characters in 2017 but that this was down from 18% in 2016 and is the lowest level recorded by GLAAD, which started the index six years ago. Who's counting? Well, GLAAD is. GLAAD's study did find some positives, including that the racial diversity of characters had improved in 2017. Well, that's good to know. Of the 109 studio films released that year, 14 featured LGBT characters, according to the Studio Responsibility Index. Of those LGBT characters, 43% were white, with 28.5% black and 28.5% Latin American. The president of GLAAD Sarah Kate Ellis said 'If Hollywood wants to remain relevant with these audiences and keep them buying tickets, they must create stories that are reflective of the world LGBTQ people and our friends and family know.'

I see. That's odd. Growing up in Ireland in the 50s and 60s, I think I might have seen just one or two films that were set in or were about Ireland during that time but I wasn't bothered by the fact that almost all the films I went to see weren't reflective of the world Irish people knew. In fact, I was quite happy that they were about fabulous and sunny locations and exciting adventures that took me out of the grey, rain-washed and humdrum world that I knew only too well. The very last thing I wanted to see was my life or any aspect of it represented on the screen. I saw my life in all its unmediated and unrepresented reality when I stepped out of the magic of the cinema into the distinctly non-magical reality of the wet and dark streets of my home town.

But the rogues and vagabonds don't have it all their own way; publishers too want to be inclusive. Penguin has hopped on the diversity and inclusion bandwagon. Its new policy declares that 'Books shape the culture of society. They inspire TV shows, films, stage shows, podcasts and more. Yet too often culture is shaped by people who come from a narrow section of society. That needs to change. Over the last few years we've worked hard to create a more inclusive and representative publishing industry. We have found new ways to break down barriers, both for authors and for future publishers - but we still have more to do.' Well done Penguin, your virtue has been proudly displayed. Much done, but still more to do. Implementing their new policy, Penguin Random House is 'looking for voices currently under-represented in books and publishing. This includes writers and illustrators from BAME (Black, Asian, Minority, Ethnic) or LGBTQ (Lesbian, Gay, Bisexual, Trans, Queer) communities, writers and illustrators with a disability, or who come from a socio-economically marginalised background.'

So, what practical form will Penguin's policy take? According to Penguin, '...our industry does not currently reflect the society we live in' so, to be more inclusive, Penguin Random House is 'removing the need for a university degree from all our jobs, introducing paid work experience and finding and nurturing new writers through our

WriteNow programme.' Well, given the lamentable state of teaching and learning in our universities, I can readily understand the removal of the necessity for a university degree. After all, better the innocent ignorance of the uncertified than the carefully nurtured ignorance of the supposedly educated. However, I suspect that that's not why the requirement for a degree is being removed. But, we might wonder, why would Penguin not also remove the necessity for the ability to be able to read and comprehend complicated texts and to write acceptable standard English. After all, a lot of people haven't got these skills and if these skills are required, then they're going to feel excluded.

But Penguin Random House isn't quite finished. We are told that 'To truly understand the impact of our actions, we need to track the diversity of our authors and colleagues ... we want our new authors and colleagues to be representative of the UK population, taking into account ethnicity, gender, sexuality, social mobility and disability.' And how, pray, is Penguin Random House going to do this? Well, helpfully, Penguin has launched what it calls an 'Inclusion Tracker' which contains, as you would expect, the usual questions on gender (not sex, never sex) and ethnicity. How you define your gender and sexual orientation are some of the more interesting questions on this tracker. On the ethnicity side, we get the usual definitionally incoherent set of possibilities: Asian or Asian British, White or Black Caribbean, White: Irish or White: British. The perspective on diversity seems somewhat more limited as it doesn't appear to track the variety of European ethnicities or Antipodean ethnicities (leaving race to one side) or the diversity created by the possession and speaking of different languages and cultures but, no doubt, Penguin will rectify these defects in time. Those of a cynical cast of mind might wonder if women writers or people with disabilities or people of non-white ethnicities really want to be held to a lower standard than male writers or non-disabled writers or white writers so that Penguin Random House can get its gender, disability and ethnicity balances up to the required PC standard—but let us ignore such cynics.

Some in the Church of England are determined not to be left behind in the running of the inclusion stakes. The Dean of St

Paul's told us in April 2018 that he thought the Church of England should lose its exemption to discrimination laws because he wasn't happy that a gay Church of England priest who had been prevented from occupying a job as a hospital chaplain had lost his appeal against that decision. He told the magazine *Christian Today*, 'We have got to come to terms with the reality of the world we're in and we're not doing that. That is why we're becoming disconnected from society.'

I see. *That's* why the Church of England is becoming ever more irrelevant—it's not culture-conforming enough! Divorce—tick; contraception—tick; abortion—tick; homosexual priests—tick; women priests—tick; women bishops—tick. I must have been misreading *Romans* 12: 2 all these years. I thought it said 'And be *not* conformed to this world: but be ye transformed by the renewing of your mind, that ye may prove what is that good, and acceptable, and perfect, will of God.' It would seem that according to the good Dean, the *not* is not only superfluous but is actually counterproductive. If only the saint who gives his name to the cathedral of which Dr Ison is the Dean had known how awkward that little *not* was going to be, he would surely have omitted it. Dr Ison went on to say, 'My view is that if there is a price to be paid for what you believe in conscience then you should pay that; you should not make other people pay the price for your conscience. That applies to abortion, to issues of sexuality and gender and right across the piste. If it is legal, decent and honest but you don't believe it is right, then you have to deal with it.' I'm not quite sure what the import of this anguished comment is but I do hope that Dr Ison himself is not, ahem, taking the piste.

If the Church of England shouldn't be allowed to discriminate on the basis of religion, should atheists be excluded from it simply because of their sincerely held belief in the non-existence of God? I am reminded of a sketch from the BBC comedy programme *Not the Nine O'Clock News*, with the intriguing title, 'The Devil: Is He all Bad?' (see YouTube 2013)

The camera zooms in on a trendy, long-haired Church of England vicar, the Rev. Lance Mountjoy, who opines, 'I think, in a sense, the Devil's had a very bad press. I mean, what *is* bad? I think modern

Christians should have a bit less of the 'Get thee behind me Satan' and more of the "Come in, me old mate, and have a cup of tea"!'

The scene then shifts to some very middle-class diabolists dressed in middle-class clothes sitting on a middle-class couch in a middle class home with the middle-class names, Fiona and George. George says, 'I don't think there is a problem, really ... ('murdering', Fiona mutters) ... 'Well, yes,' George concedes, 'except for the murdering. The modern day diabolist, I mean we're not really mumbo-jumbo Dennis Wheatley types ... ' ('Coffee mornings,' Fiona interjects, 'bring-and-buy sales ...') The interviewer is somewhat taken aback by this rather humdrum suburban description of diabolism. 'Bring-and-buy sales!' he asks, incredulously. George clarifies: 'Well, I say bring-and-buy sales, it's more sort of murdering, actually ... (Fiona interjects, 'virgins') ...well, yes, rape, coffee ...'

The scene shifts back to our Lance, who is reclining semi-recumbently outside the door of a church. 'Well, yes, what *is* a virgin? I've never met one! [He laughs.] No, but seriously. Yeah, yeah, cautiously, cautiously, I would approve of sacrificing the odd virgin. Mmmm, I mean, fair enough' The interviewer wonders what devil worshippers actually believe? Fiona obliges. 'Well, we believe that Satan, the Prince of Darkness is Lord of the Universe and will destroy Jesus through infernal power.' Back once again to Lance, who says, 'Yeah, obviously, this is a difficult one! It's a theological grey area, but I think we should keep a broad outlook, after all, intrinsically, the roots of all religions are the same. Buddhism is hardly different from Christianity, and Muslims are exactly the same as Christians, only with more money.'

What do our devil worshippers actually get up to? George obligingly explains: 'Well, every full moon, we do go up to the Heath at midnight, and we do strip ourselves completely naked, and we ravish each other passionately till dawn.' The interviewer, his interest picking up, asks 'And this helps summon up the forces of evil, does it?' George replies, 'Who cares?'

Will the diabolist Fionas and Georges of this world ever be accepted by the Church of England? 'Bound to happen, bound to happen,' says Lance. 'In my opinion, it won't be too long before devil worshippers are accepted into the priesthood. Some people are going to oppose it—the Pope, I think, is probably anti—but it's on the cards, yeah.' The interviewer puts the same question to Fiona and George: 'Do you think you will finally be accepted into the Church?' to which George responds with the sublimely deflationary, 'I couldn't give a toss!' And who shall blame you for not giving a toss, George, who shall blame you?

Cultural Appropriation
One hot topic closely related to the DIE-versity Dogma is that of cultural appropriation. 'Cultural appropriation' as now defined in the *Cambridge Dictionary* is 'the act of taking or using things from a culture that is not your own, especially without showing that you understand or respect this culture.' Well, now that it's in the dictionary, I suppose we must accept that there is such a thing as cultural appropriation; on the other hand, perhaps not.

There are a number of problematic things about this concept. Cultural appropriation presupposes that there are distinct cultures which are, as it were, hermetically sealed off from one another and in which there can be identified elements that belong exclusively to each particular culture so that their use or employment in another culture constitutes a kind of misappropriation or theft. It has been said that imitation is the sincerest form of flattery which would seem to make borrowing elements of another culture rather a mark of esteem or respect rather than otherwise. A small point that is perhaps worth mentioning—cultural appropriation either works in all directions or it doesn't work at all. So come on Bach Collegium Japan, stop singing and recording the Bach Cantatas; all you non-European peoples wearing suits and trousers, please remove them; and all you non-native English speakers had better cease and desist from misappropriating that language, language surely being among the chief products of any culture.

Allen Farrington tells of a friend of his from Singapore who, while studying at the University of Edinburgh, joined the University's Black and Minority Ethnic Liberation Group. Unfortunately, his friend discovered that it's not enough to be Black or a member of a minority ethnic group to belong to such an august body; you must also think the right thoughts. His friend came to grief on the rocks of cultural appropriation when he denied the very validity of the concept. He pointed out that nobody can own a culture (and so it can't be appropriated) but that even if it *were* possible to steal it, this very peculiar form of theft doesn't actually remove it from the hands of its original putative owners! Moreover, he pointed out that cultural exchange had been an important factor in human progress and that it had helped to defuse bigotry. For his pains, he was told that expressing such delinquent thoughts was triggering and offensive and made people of colour feel unsafe and so he was ejected from the group. (see Farrington)

Though cultural appropriation has thrust itself upon our attention relatively recently, it isn't something that started only yesterday. Here's a little something from the dim and distant days of the last millennium which shows an embryonic form of cultural appropriation in action. In an essay she published in 1994, Professor Katherine Mayberry tells us a cautionary tale. (Mayberry 1994) She attended a conference at which she was to present a paper on Toni Morrison's *Beloved*. All the participants on that panel were white women, with the exception of the moderator. When the moderator had introduced the participants, she indicated her intention of leaving the room because, she said, she wasn't comfortable with the 'appropriation' of black literature by white women. She was not interested in anything that white women had to say about the literature produced by black writers. Professor Mayberry's first reaction was the normal one of indignation that the views of the intended presenters could be pre-emptively rejected simply on the grounds of race. But she quickly got over this reactionary attitude and moved to acquire the proper state of liberal guilt for failing to realise the cruel irony of middle-class white women claiming to explain and interpret a powerful slave narrative.

The canon of cultural appropriateness appears to be that not only should you write about what you have experienced but you should *not* write or even comment on what you have not experienced. Would it be rude of me to point out that black feminists have had no more experience of slavery than white feminists and so are just as much prohibited from writing or commenting about slavery by the canon of cultural appropriateness unless one thinks (why?)

that only people who possess a certain skin colour can write about people with approximately the same skin colour who were at one time slaves. As a leader-writer in *The New Criterion* says, 'For Professor Mayberry ... the traditional goals of scholarship—responsible interpretation and explanation—must give way to the mysticism of an "authentic response" in which one's sex or race or ethnic origin determines the nature of one's access to knowledge.' (Anon. 1994)

The old dictum of sticking to writing about what you know has taken a new twist in the age of cultural appropriation. Now, you can write only about what you are! So, whites are not allowed to have black characters in their novels or short stories—to do so would be artificial and patronising. Of course, by parity of reasoning, the old shouldn't write about the young (or *vice versa*), men about women, women about men, and so on. In the end, taken to its logical conclusion, the only person a writer can write about without committing the dreaded sin of cultural appropriation is—himself! But isn't art, well, artificial? And isn't that the whole point of it?

The shtick of cultural appropriation is the artistic version of what has been called 'insider epistemology' which is the absurd idea that you can know something only if you have the right credentials. So, only blacks can know about black experience—note, not *have* black experience which is self-evidently true, but know about it, which is not self-evidently true. So too, only women can know about female experience—once again, not have it, which is a truism, but know about it, which isn't a truism.

But as Allen Farrington's friend pointed out, the whole idea of ownership in relation to cultural items is nonsense. The proper response to this nonsense is to write about whatever you want to write about, paint whatever you want to paint in whatever way you want to paint it. The only criterion—the *only* criterion—relevant to what you write or paint is whether it is any good, whether it's worth reading or looking at. The same goes for music, hair styles, and clothes. The sex, skin colour, sexual orientation, and cultural affiliation of the person who wrote it or painted it is supremely irrelevant.

Sometimes, the disputes over cultural appropriation centre on the essence of triviality. In one case in 2017, a hairstylist salon that operates out of the high-end London store Selfridges was accused of cultural appropriation because it offered braided plaits. It seems that the particular hairstyle in question has been worn exclusively by black women and men for centuries. Ah yes, a hairstyle that belongs exclusively to a particular culture—remarkable! Braided hairstyles, one complainer whined, are 'so near and dear to a marginalised community' that it was a travesty that the hairstyles were 'being taken from them'. Really, if A gets her hair braided, this somehow prevents B from doing so too. It's a zero-sum game. Who would have thought it?

In Australia, *Meanjin*, the literary quarterly, hopped on the MeToo bandwagon by changing the 'Me' element in its logo to 'MeToo' and striking through the 'anjin' bit in an effort to demonstrate its woke credentials. What could possibly be wrong with that? Well, you see, *Meanjin* is the Turrbal word for what became Brisbane and the change apparently caused anguish among those to whom this word and its associations are sacred. Some indigenous women said that it felt 'weird' to see *Meanjin* crossed out because the 'destruction of land, cultures and language is fundamentally tied to violence against Aboriginal women'. It looked as if our sensitive name changers at the quarterly were prioritising feminist issues over aboriginal ones only to offend feminist aboriginal sensibilities in so doing!

Cue grovelling apologies! 'The Devil made us to it,' said the editorial staff. Well, not quite. Not the Devil, but whiteness and white privilege the latter-day equivalent of diabolical influence. White shame is an inverted example of white pride. 'Look,' it says, 'look how bad, how transcendently bad, we are.' It's a little like the monk who was proud to boast 'I'm the most modest monk in this monastery!' Jonathan Green, editor of *Meanjin*, said, 'I should therefore have known better. We work with words; the power of this erasure should not have been lost on us. He continued, 'It's a reminder that the human stocks of this magazine could be enhanced by a broader range of backgrounds and mindsets in the editorial process.' Human stocks? Does he mean people? He might just as well have written, 'I'm white. Help! *Mea culpa, mea culpa, mea ultima culpa.*' All those whites and non-whites seem to be playing a very old game, one that not so long ago seemed to be superseded. Whites, adults with all the power, must be careful not to hurt the fragile non-whites who are, it seems, ultra-sensitive and not quite rational children. The original change to the logo wasn't racist, just plain stupid, but the apology *was* racist, implying a difference in emotional fragility between the races, with whites as permanent aggressors and non-whites as permanent helpless emotionally unstable victims.

Works of art are now regularly examined to make sure their cultural credentials are in order and that nasty cultural appropriators aren't going around looting other people's cultural goods. Some people have objected to a painting that depicted black suffering on the grounds that it was painted by a white artist. A Canadian painter had an exhibition cancelled because her work was based on a style used by Anishinable artists. Whatever you do, don't use points of paint to make your art-work, for that technique is reserved for native Australian artists. ('Tell that to the pointillists of the early 20th century!) Damien Hirst, doyen of the so-called Young British Artists, is just one artist who has been accused of committing the new mortal sin of cultural appropriation. One indigenous Australian artist has said that she is hurt that Hirst might have copied the paintings of her people in a series of works called *The Veil Paintings* exhibited at the Gagosian Gallery in Los Angeles in 2018. These paintings, it seems, make use of spots or points and that, it seems, is something to which indigenous Australians have an exclusive right. Barbara Weir, who is a traditional Australian painter, said that Hirst's works bore a striking resemblance to the work of her aunt and those of Emily Kame Kngwarreye. Bronwyn Bancroft, another indigenous artist and an Arts Law Centre board member, also told ABC News she believed it was 'obvious' that Hirst's work had been influenced by Aboriginal art. 'I was a little bit shocked,' she said, 'when I saw them 'cause I thought they could have been passed [off] as some Utopian work.' She went on to say, 'You can't actually copyright style ... [but] in many ways it's what's called a moral copyright element.' Moral copyright, eh! There's an interestingly absurd idea. Hirst, on the other hand, said that his paintings were inspired by the French Post-Impressionists Seurat and Bonnard which doesn't make them better or worse than if they had been copied from Australian sources, just derivative.

Ms Weir was hurt because artists shouldn't be doing something that belongs to someone else. What exactly is it that belongs to someone else? She suggested that Mr Hirst, if he did copy the work of her aunt and other indigenous artists, had no right to do so. A spokeswoman for Hirst denied that he was aware of the work of the artist in question or even of the artist but was quick to make the usual soothing PC noises about his respect for the importance of art in all cultures.

Even those who are most woke can find themselves in trouble if they cross the red line of cultural appropriation. For example, Dana Schultz painted a portrait of the lynched Emmett Till that was exhibited at the Whitney Biennial in New York in 2017. One African-American artist called for the painting's removal and destruction on the grounds that it isn't acceptable for a white person to transmute black suffering into profit and fun. Schultz protested that not being black she didn't know what it was like to be black in America, she did however know what it was like to be a mother. Her protest was unavailing. She was told that the subject matter was not hers. Hannah Black wrote that 'White free speech and white creative freedom have been founded on the constraint of others and are not natural rights. The painting must go.' She also contended that 'contemporary art is a fundamentally white supremacist institution despite all our nice friends.' (see Kennedy 2017)

The phrase used by Black, 'The subject matter is not Schulz's' is revealing. It makes the story of the lynching of Emmett Till to be a matter of some kind of property, the property that accrues to and only to those who share his skin colour. But this is absurd. My skin colour doesn't give me some unique insight into and ownership over things that have happened to or been done by other white people, any more than my height (5' 11") gives me some kind of solidarity with all those who have tried and failed to reach 6'. Would it be considered wildly radical to suggest that stories don't belong to anyone. Even I don't have a propriety interest or sole right to the story of my own life. If I tell it, it is just me telling my story. Others can tell it if they wish and may, in fact, tell it better than I can.

What could possibly be wrong with the Brooklyn Museum's having a curator of African Art? Nothing, you might think. Think again. When in 2018 Kristen Windmuller-Luna was announced as its new curator, the protests began. Why? Isn't she one of those flawlessly perfect human beings, a woman? What could there possibly be to protest about? Well, you see, she's—how can I say it without blushing—she's white! If that isn't cultural appropriation, nothing is! Not only that, it's a perpetuation of colonialist attitudes on the part of the Museum.

The protestors want Ms Windmuller-Luna to be replaced, of course, but that's not all. It seems that the structures of the art world are pervaded by white supremacy and that too must change. Ms Windmuller's replacement by a more suitable candidate is only the first step. After that, progress must be made in the decolonisation project. First, it must be admitted that the Museum itself stands on land stolen from Indigenous people, that many if not most of its objects were stolen from non-white people and, of course, that those who run the institution are largely white.

In a way parallel to the appropriation of culture, it seems that we can have the appropriation of personal experiences. Morgan Jones, writing in *The Guardian* in August 2018, believes that as a 47 year old man who has never lived outside the UK, he has to justify his writing from the perspective of a 17 year old girl from Cairo. He says that he has been asked, 'What gives you the right to write this story?' He thinks that's a good question. I think it's a bloody stupid and impertinent question.

Jones is sympathetic to the idea that doing what he is doing could be construed as an act of presumption or exploitation, usurping the culture, experience and identity of people who are never heard, robbing people of their own voices. On the other hand, in a moment of common sense, he acknowledges that if a writer is confined to writing about what he knows, he'll ultimately be confined to writing about himself and nothing else and what, with respect, could be more boring than that, the perfect inversion of Hitchcock's epigram that 'Cinema is just like ordinary life with all the boring bits left out.' So, he puzzles, if we want to extend beyond the limits of ourselves, how far can we go and who decides that? He wonders if, as a *man*, he can write a female character, or a gay character, or a person from a different class. What he should be wondering of course is if, as a *writer*, he can write a female character or a gay character or a person from a different class. Fiction writing is an act of imagination and the only limits on what you can write are your ability to harness the power of your imagination and your ability to find a publisher and, if you're very lucky, some readers.

In the end, Jones comes down firmly in the middle of the road, a dangerous place to be, since you're likely to be killed by traffic coming from both directions. On the one hand, he accepts that novelists have to use their imaginations; on the other, he accepts that this is an invasive process that involves a degree of appropriation, perhaps even theft! Invasive process? Who or what is being invaded? And appropriation? What does that mean? In the end, since Jones is only a novelist, his ruminations on invasion and appropriation might be taken by the uninitiated to be a sign rather of megalomania than of modesty.

❧

Diversity in the University

This place is the Devil, or at least his principal residence,
they call it the University, but any other appellation
would have suited it much better, for study is the
last pursuit of the society; the Master eats, drinks, and
sleeps, the Fellows drink, dispute and pun, the employments of the
undergraduates you will probably conjecture without my description
—Lord Byron

Ideological diversity is not welcome in our universities

The extraordinary events that are reported as occurring on college campuses primarily in the Anglophone world are often portrayed as if they were just local and idiosyncratic eruptions of the febrile student mind or the actions of well-intentioned if somewhat over-exuberant activists in the promotion of causes that are, in themselves, honourable and just. That's not quite what is happening. What is in fact taking place on campuses are battles in a broader culture war between, on the one hand, science and other disciplines where there is a residual respect for truth, evidence and reason, and, on the other hand, post-modernism, where truth is merely a myth masking ideological power grabs and ideas are merely weapons in the advancement or retardation of liberal social goals. Postmodernism and its bastard offspring—critical race theory, critical legal theory et al.—accord priority to lived experience as the primary if not the only source of knowledge. Reality is not something to which our knowledge must conform but, godlike as the postmodernists are (at least in their own estimation), reality must rather conform itself to their knowledge. The biggest casualty of all in the contemporary university is its commitment to the pursuit of truth. This is largely because the presuppositions behind that commitment, that there is a truth to be discovered and that reason is the way to that truth, are now themselves matters of contention.

Scientists and engineers are particularly prone to subscribe to the naïve belief that there is a truth to be discovered rather than invented and that reality is what it is and not what we happen to make it to be. In particular, when it comes to human beings, biologists have a distressing tendency to think that men and women are biologically diverse and to use quasi-racist terms such as *genetic* as if they corresponded to a reality that is fundamentally independent of our human minds! Besieged in their academic redoubts, still dedicated to the discovery and to the propagation of truth, once their scientific outposts are overrun, the victory of postmodernism in the academy will be complete. These intransigent holdouts must be brought to heel in this brave, new world of diversity and some progress has been made in that direction. While academics in the STEM subjects (science, technology, engineering and mathematics) are for the most part unscathed by the postmodern revolution, though not wholly so, with a few honourable exceptions, most of the academic staff in the humanities, social sciences and law are already firmly on board with the postmodern agenda and don't need to be proselytised or coerced. In these disciplines, these truths are universally acknowledged: that the sexes are interchangeable and that gender is fluid, that there are no ethical absolutes, that logic and rationality are tools of the patriarchy and that politics is nothing more than the acquisition, retention and employment of power. (Ignore the seeming paradox that there can be truths while yet there is no truth!) To question these doctrines is, from the perspective of the new *illuminati*, not just wrong-headed and foolish but evil and perverse.

The shocking thing to someone like myself, a child of the 60s, is that the new orthodoxies are being imposed not just by the academic staff but also by the students. Anyone offering a deviant line is quickly brought to heel by the relativist attack (that's just *your* point of view) and, if persistent, attacked by an 'ism' or a 'phobia' ('You can't say that: that's racism, sexism, homophobia, transphobia.') Professors and lecturers who dare to continue to deviate are not exempt from the terrorism of the student mob. (see again

Nayna 2019 & 2019a and Anon. 2017; and for some rampant campus insanity and eye-watering administrative pusillanimity, watch the video at Anon. 2017.)

The attack on the universality of truth is closely linked to the increasing emotional hyper-sensitivity of contemporary students. If truth is inherently perspectival then it becomes *my* truth and when you question my truth, it is my very being that is being challenged. Intellectual conflict thus becomes ineluctably personal. Moreover, if there is no reality that can discriminate between truth or falsity or better or worse views, however difficult it may be to access it, then argument becomes simply a form of intellectual violence and persuasion just a thinly-veiled form of force.

A prime example of the rejection of traditional intellectual values is the current craze for diversity in the universities. Universities are appointing diversity officers as fast as they can find them; there is even a National Association of Diversity Officers in Higher Education! Governments and corporations are leaning heavily in that direction as well. As many as one fifth of Fortune 500 companies employ a diversity officer. What do these Diversity Officers do? According to one source, Diversity Officers help to maintain a diverse workforce, which, it tells us, is recognised as key to a successful business and they do this by reducing workplace discrimination on the grounds of age, disability, gender, race, religion and sexual orientation. That all looks pretty harmless, doesn't it? Who could be in favour of discrimination, after all? But the diversity dogma is not a harmless academic eccentricity but an fifth-column attack on the fundamental values of the university.

In some US university campuses, faculty members are required to make a statement of faith in diversity. Some twenty major universities including the University of California and Carnegie-Mellon University, require diversity statements when it comes to hiring or promotion. At UCLA, anyone hoping for tenure is/was required to write an essay, giving an account of the efforts he or she was/ is making to remediating the racial and gender imbalances in his/ her/its department. Out with statements of faith in Methodism or Evangelicalism—in with the statements of faith in diversity; out with respect for the individual, for merit, for achievement, for ignoring incidentals of race and ethnicity and language—in with the assignment of merit and demerit on the basis of group membership. No longer is it enough to be hired or to be promoted that you have the appropriate qualifications, a good teaching record and respectable publications; now, you must also publicly commit yourself to the promotion of diversity. No commitment to diversity, no hiring, no promotion.

Representational diversity in the academy is sometimes justified on the grounds that it leads to better results all round in the intellectual life, and that's only when someone actually bothers to offer a justification. Excellence, it seems, just isn't possible without diversity, at least, that's what Columbia's Vice Provost Dennis Mitchell thinks. What is the evidence for this non-self-evident claim? Somehow, without having the kind of diversity that Mitchell sees as necessary for excellence, staff members at Columbia have managed, miraculously it would seem, to win 78 Nobel prizes in the sciences and in economics. I suppose Mitchell might retort, 'Ah yes, but just think how many more they would have won if they had been a more diverse group.' Hmmmm.

What kind of diversity is Mitchell talking about? It can't be diversity in thinking unless he's making the bizarre point that non-male non-white people think significantly differently in, say, science or engineering! Do the so-called underrepresented females and minorities think or solve problems in a uniquely different way from other people? Does mathematics work differently because of your sex or your skin colour? Given that so-called progressive thinkers believe that gender (sex) and race are socially constructed anyway, why then would females and underrepresented minorities think differently if their alleged differences are simply the outcome of oppressive social categories?

One conservative academic said that 'all too often faculty and administrators want people of different races, ethnicity and gender thinking the same things.' Surely that can't be true! If it's not, then what do we make of what the website *College Factual* has to say about diversity: 'When most students seek diversity on campus, what they are looking for are opportunities to express themselves and find community with others who believe the same way, as well as opportunities to learn from those from different cultures and backgrounds.' What is interesting is what is missing from this vignette. 'The university years,' the report rhapsodises, 'provide a one of a kind opportunity for students to have exposure to other backgrounds and cultures.' Exposure to backgrounds and cultures, yes, but not, it would seem, exposure to other beliefs. There is diversity and then there is diversity. Diversity in though is not only *not* celebrated but we are told that what students are looking for is to find community 'with others *who believe the same way...*' (see College Factual)

The *desideratum*, then, is diversity, diversity in everything but thought; different races, different ethnicities, different ages, different sexualities, but no real difference in thinking. When it comes to thinking, orthodoxy is required and especially obedience to the new great commandments: thou shalt love and promote diversity with all thy heart and all thy mind and all thy soul and all thy strength and thou shalt love thy neighbour as thyself—unless he is a racist, a homophobe, a sexist, a transphobe or just a white man. The idea that human beings are human beings first and everything else afterwards is not a form of intellectual diversity that can be tolerated. Neither is the idea that groups have little or no moral significance and shouldn't be the basis for legislation or policy. Neither is the idea that the most fundamental practical form of equality in a free society is equality before the law. Diversityology is essentially anti-liberal in its rejection of universalism, legal equality and, I would add, the importance of the individual's not being subsumed into groups, either for advantage or for disadvantage.

Campus diversity in the UK

Is Britain going to go the same way as the USA by introducing quotas in education for minorities to achieve some kind of pre-determined ratio? The idea of diversity has gained so much traction that to suggest that we might select candidates for jobs or university places on the basis of their demonstrated achievements and qualifications is taken to be tantamount to some kind of covert racism!

Allow me introduce you to the wonderful world of the UK's Equality Challenge Unit (ECU)! Never heard of it? Why should you? The ECU was born in 2005 and is alive and well and living in London. With a staff of around 40, it receives funds from pretty much every university in the UK. It sponsors two charters—a Race Equality Charter (REC), and a gender-equality charter with the charming name of Athena Swan (AS). Universities and university departments that meet certain criteria can be awarded these charters. It all sounds innocent enough—after all, who could be against equality!—but its effects are none the less malign for all that. Do you think that the purpose of a university is to teach students, conduct research in the sciences and the humanities? Well, think again, you poor deluded fool! Now the promotion of equality and diversity is a goal of the university all by its very own self and the ECU is here to make sure that we all get on board with the programme.

Indeed, the ECU isn't just concerned with traditional 'fair treatment' equality, the sort no one could object to. Instead it goes a good deal further. What articles of faith does a university have to subscribe to in order to receive an ECU charter? Take the Race Equality Charter, which universities are under almost irresistible peer pressure to adopt. If a university wants to participate, its Vice-Chancellor must formally endorse a document stating, among other things, that racism is an everyday facet of UK society and that diverse teams enhance creativity and promote innovation. For an Athena Swan award, the process is similar. Any university signing up to it must commit itself to 'addressing unequal gender representation across academic disciplines and professional and support functions ... making and mainstreaming sustainable structural and cultural changes to advance gender equality, recognising that initiatives and actions that support individuals alone will not sufficiently advance equality ... [and] tackling the discriminatory treatment often experienced by trans people'.

Staying in Britain, a UK government-funded scheme is to be introduced in which, in a daring reversal of the usual norm of the young being mentored by the old, senior white academics will instead be assigned a junior female colleague from an ethnic minority as a mentor to enable what are sometimes patronisingly called 'male, stale and pale' professors to confront their biases. Let's present the presuppositions of this astonishingly sexist, ageist and racist mentoring scheme in the starkest fashion: old, white, male = bad; young, non-white and female = good. The person overseeing the project at Birmingham University, Professor John Rowe, said that he hoped that the scheme would permit eminent professors to confront their biases. Quite how he knows that they have these biases is not entirely clear but Professor Rowe somehow knows that we've all got them. I see. By the way, does that include Professor Rowe himself? Does that also include the junior female colleagues from ethnic minorities or are they somehow magically exempt from such biases? If they're not, why aren't *their* biases being challenged? Somewhat more opaquely, Professor Rowe tells us that 'While it is well known and obvious that women and minority groups suffer setbacks to their career progression no one really understands why.' Leaving to one side the non-obvious claim that women and minority groups suffer setbacks to their career progression (Do they? Is it in some way different from the setbacks suffered by anyone else?) to the extent that this is so I thought we were to believe that was the result of this invisible but omnipresent bias? Is that not so after all?

Is there any, ahem, actual evidence, apart from the disparities in proportions to justify the claim of prejudice and to justify institutionalising overt biases in favour of such allegedly discriminated-against groups? Professor Rowe again: 'It's not as if there is any overt prejudice—it is something to do with the way the system is or the way it has evolved and we needed to find out why.' Ah, I see! Well, actually, no I don't. It seems that it's not individuals who are at fault, it's the system, whatever *that* may be! This nonsense is prompted by the usual claim that women and ethnic minority academics are under-represented at the top levels of the academy, a kind of representation that, as I've already pointed out, is intrinsically nonsensical. One very practical thing that the fellow-travelling white, male perpetrators of this ridiculous notion such as Professor Rowe could do to advance the cause of diversity is to resign their own positions to diverse others, whites to blacks, men to women, able-bodied to disabled, but don't hold your breath.

What we have here, apart from the usual reverse sexism and racism is a large chunk of junk science. What is this mysterious thing called 'unconscious bias' (UB) that Professor Rowe claims to be able to detect and how is it supposed to manifest itself? If the disparate outcomes for diverse groups are the phenomena to be explained and unconscious bias is postulated as the causal source of these outcomes, the disparate outcomes cannot be used as evidence to support the assertion of UB as its cause. It's as if the argument ran: 'We've got a bad case of UB in our universities. Really? What's the evidence for this? Well, we've got disparate outcomes for diverse groups. Yes, let's accept that as an empirical fact, but how do you know that the cause of the diverse outcomes is UB? Well, we've got diverse outcomes? Yes, I know that. What *independent* evidence is there to support the claim that the cause is UB?' Ummmm....

A professor at Oxford was told in 2016 that he must retire on diversity grounds in order to safeguard the high standards of the university and to allow for inter-generational fairness. (Anon. 2018a) Professor John Pitcher claims that he was forcibly retired by the university on the basis of what is called an Employment Justified Retirement Age (EJRA) policy. Oxford's EJRA is designed to promote what the University thinks of as inter-generational fairness and improvements in diversity. Global mandatory retirement ages were, if I may so phrase it, retired in 2010, and the EJRA is the re-introduction of a form of local mandatory retirement. In 2012, Professor Pitcher's retirement date was set for Sept 30 2016 but he was then made a Founder's Fellow on a fixed term from 2014 to 2020. In 2016 he was told his employment wouldn't be extended to 2020. He took an action against the college and university for unfair dismissal, alleging discrimination on the grounds of age. Professor Pitcher noted that of the so-called Russell Group of universities, only Cambridge has kept a retirement age, and he argued that 'None of these other institutions have reduced their standards by not forcibly retiring staff. There is no evidence to support the need to 'refresh' the academic workforce in terms of turnover.' As I write (May 2019), Professor Pitcher has just lost his suit against the university. He has the right to appeal but the end of this story extends beyond the limits of this book. The principal of Brasenose College, John Bowers QC, said that the ruling provided 'a thorough vindication of the University and College position to have a retirement age' and he remarked that 'There is a strong feeling that the only way to keep refreshing the diversity of the academic community is to keep a retirement age.' Out with the old, the white and the male; in with the young, the female and the BAME.

But despite the best efforts of the enlightened ones, problems with diversity and inclusion appear to persist. 'Most people involved in the delivery of history, in universities, publishing, museums and the heritage industry, are aware that we have a problem with diversity and inclusivity.' So writes David Olusoga. (Olusoga 2018) He treats us to the exhibition of the percentage of BAME in the general population and the percentage of BAME in universities and history departments. (BAME is sometimes shortened to BME.) 15% of academics are BAME but only 6.3% of people in history departments are BAME. Only 0.5% of history academics are black whereas black people comprise 3% of the UK's population. The result of all this, according to Mr Olusoga, is that black students are rejecting history as a subject that is attractive to them. Really? Even taking these figures as a given, where's the evidence for Mr Olusoga's conclusion here? Correlation, as we all know, does not by itself prove causation.

It has been argued that students need to see people like themselves (that is to say, like themselves in respect of race or sex) on the lecture podium. But why should this be so? As a woman, do you *necessarily* teach other women better than a man? Does your being a woman just as such aid your female students to learn in a way that would not be possible if you were a man? Does a female student really think that her instructor needs to be female if she is to learn well or think that if her instructor is male, she is somehow debarred from pursuing a career in her STEM discipline? How did Marie Curie manage, one wonders? Please explain? Substitute race for sex and you get the same point. Would your students equally appreciate seeing someone of their own *age* in front of them instead of someone usually considerably older, or someone from their own part of the country, or someone from their own town, or someone from their own street? Why limit the 'like can learn only from like' principle (to give it a dignity it doesn't deserve) merely to race and sex? On the other hand, you could just be happy that you've got the best-qualified person teaching you, whatever that person's race or sex or point of geographical origin.

Another thing that people like Mr Olusoga seem to know is that women and minorities are underrepresented in STEM disciplines. Of course, as I've already pointed out, the notion of representation as employed in this context makes no sense but that doesn't stop anyone from using it as a weapon of mass destruction. Given that every school or department in the university is engaged in a battle to improve its rankings, it would make virtually no sense, indeed it would be self-destructive, for any school or department to ignore the best-qualified potential staff members or researchers because of some antipathy to a candidate's race or sex. This is similar to the myth of the gender pay gap. If equally qualified and experienced women were consistently prepared to work for a lower salary than comparably qualified and experienced men, then an employer would have to be seriously economically irrational to employ anyone else but women! It is a commonplace to think that women are disadvantaged when it comes to applying for university positions in STEM subjects but the reality is that being a woman in today's new normative environment is a distinct advantage!

Those promoting diversity bemoan the fact that almost all of those in senior university administration positions are non-BMEs, only 3%, in fact, while the national baseline for BMEs is 13%. Please note again what should be by now the very familiar and seemingly unshiftable assumption that there should be a correlation between the ratio of entity X in some specific area of employment or education and the ratio of entity X in the general population.

Some BMEs in universities complain that they are tired of having to succeed against the odds or of being considered not quite ready for promotion or of being mistaken for the cleaner or of seeing appointments that are said to be made on merit being obviously discriminatory. Would it be unkind of me to point out that having to succeed against the odds or not being quite ready for promotion are experiences familiar to almost *all* academics, most of them non-BMEs. And if you dress like a slob, as most academics and students do, it's no wonder if you are taken for the cleaner— it would be much more surprising if you weren't. And how would one know, without specific evidence, that a particular appointment said to be made on merit was *not* made on merit but was discriminatory? When one is not hired or not promoted, it is quite understandable that one is disappointed. Often, one has the feeling that the process or the outcome was unfair; this is so whether one is BME or non-BME. But that disappointment, however real and painful, is not in itself evidence of discrimination. What *would* be evidence of discrimination would be to show that Candidate A, who was appointed or promoted, was significantly less qualified along the normal academic parameters of publications, degrees, teaching experience etc. than Candidate B who wasn't? Feelings of discrimination, however deep and significant they may be to a particular human being, are not in and by themselves evidence of discrimination.

Campus diversity in the USA

So much for Britain. What of the USA? In July 2018, as part of a broader purge of guidelines issued by prior US administrations, the Attorney General Jeff Sessions rescinded six guidance documents that had been issued under the Obama administration between 2011 and 2016 that encouraged universities to take a student's race into account to promote diversity in admissions. Mr Session said the guidelines were 'unnecessary, outdated, inconsistent with existing law, or otherwise improper'. These guidance documents—guidance only in the sense that failure to comply with them would draw down on any institution failing to implement them the ire of the relevant US funding agencies—had argued that, in the interests of diversity, universities could lawfully take race into account in coming to their decisions on admission. This use of race was justified on the grounds that third level institutions had what was called a 'compelling interest' in obtaining the benefits that would follow from having a diverse student body. Among the material contained in those documents, there are some whose truth is, shall we say, incapable of being verified. For example, these guidance documents confidently assert that 'Learning environments comprised of students from diverse backgrounds provide an enhanced educational experience for individual students.' It cannot be doubted that diversity of various kinds will provide *some* kind of experience for students but there is no compelling evidence that such experience will necessarily be *educational*. Another assertion is that, 'By choosing to create this kind of rich academic environment, educational institutions help students sharpen their critical thinking and analytical skills.' Once again, this claim is scarcely self-evidently true and it is difficult to see what kind of empirical evidence could be adduced to support it. By withdrawing the affirmative action guidance of previous administrations, the current US administration is promoting race-blind admissions processes instead of encouraging universities in a kind of the-king's-wish-is-my-command kind of way to consider an applicant's race. As I write, the US Justice Department is investigating Harvard over allegations of racial discrimination in respect of admissions and has asked the university to disclose its admission practices. In the larger context of premier universities, a scandal has erupted over what would appear to be a kind of admissions-for-cash policy. The investigation of this phenomenon is ongoing.

A lawsuit has been filed against Harvard currently by the Students for Fair Admissions which alleges that the University holds Asian-American applicants to an unfairly high admissions standard. White and Asian students have to score much higher on the SAT exams—anywhere from 310-450 points!—to have the same chance of being admitted as black students. It seems patently obvious but not so to everyone that to make it more difficult for students of a particular race to achieve something than for students of a different race is, not to put too fine a point on it, racist. One common response to this charge of reverse racism is to argue that such affirmative action is only for the short term until the systemic advantages that one group (whites) have had is eliminated and then we can revert to race blindness. The trouble with this assertion is that it's false—it's been fifty years of so since affirmative action was first introduced, sufficient time, one would think, to eliminate systemic disadvantages, assuming any such to have existed. Moreover, it's fundamentally unjust to disadvantage a particular individual because of the perceived injustice done by the race of which he is a member, just as it is unjust to reward a member of a race that has been the object of a perceived injustice. This is collectivism at its most naked. Groups don't have rights—individuals do, and when individuals are punished or rewarded for being members of a particular race, this is, all special pleading to one side, racism. And this is not even to begin to try to get your head around the idea that Asian students, who could reasonably claim to have been systematically disadvantaged because of the way in which their racial groups were historically treated, are now systematically disadvantaged as if they or their progenitors had somehow belonged to the supposedly oppressing group! On the face of it, it seems as if Harvard's admission policy is systematically biased against Asian-American students. If academic merit was taken into account, then the proportion of such students in first-tier universities would go from something like 19% to 43%! It seems that the reason for their proportionately lower admission rates—and this would be funny if the outcomes were not so serious—is that they tend to score lower in such personality traits as courage or kindness!

There was (and may still be) an old adage in legal circles, when in doubt, deny, deny, deny, and the supporters of affirmative action by whatever name it is called consistently deny that affirmative action is essentially racist despite its being obvious that it is so. In the end, the really sad thing about policies of diversity and inclusion and all their works and pomps is that they keep race at the forefront of our thought so that it becomes ever more difficult to transcend matters of skin colour and to evaluate individual human beings by their characters and achievements.

But it is not only the members of excluded groups who are hurt by such skewed admission policies. There are also unfortunate side-effects to this kind of policy for the members of the supposedly disadvantaged groups, not all of whom, by the way, support such policies. Some intended beneficiaries are not even members of oppressed groups! About 10 years ago, it turned out that half of black students in Harvard were not, in fact, descendants of Americans slaves but the offspring of recent immigrants! A 2016 Gallup poll revealed that 57% of blacks agreed with the statement that race or ethnicity 'should not be a factor at all' in the college admissions process and another poll conducted for the *Washington Post* found that 86% of blacks agreed that decisions about hiring and admissions 'should be based strictly on merit and qualifications other than race/ethnicity,' even if the goal of a preferential policy would be to 'give minorities more opportunity'. Those from such a group who are admitted to a first-tier university will be suspected of having gained access by having had lower standards applied to them than were applied to other groups whether such is the case or not. This is decidedly unjust to individuals from such groups who have attained their positions by virtue of their academic achievements Moreover, if you place people in an environment for which they are not fitted by their abilities, then you are likely to meet problems downstream if, as is distinctly possible, such individuals are unable to cope with the academic demands that are made of them. Do you then continue with a policy of lower standards in such instances? It's hard to see how this could be sustained when such individuals emerge into the real world, the world of medicine, engineering, business, finance. But who cares if the policy works when, in the end, it's really a matter of virtue signalling.

   And in any case, just who is diverse, who is not diverse? What do these questions even mean? In Joshua Harmon's play *Admissions*, these are the type of questions that drive the plot. Sherri Rosen-Mason (the double-barrelled name is a rather nice piece of virtue signalling!) who is the dean of admissions at an elite private school in New Hampshire and the kind of person who has nightmares about how to make the student body at her school more diverse (she's already got it up to 18% from a mere 6%) has the unpleasant experience of seeing her own son Charlie rejected by Yale while Charlie's less academically qualified pal Perry gets in. You see, Perry is half-black or, rather, his mother is white and his father is biracial which makes him .... well, I'm not quite sure what it makes him but whatever that is, it's less white than Charlie. Wasn't this kind of racial arithmetic the kind of thing we were supposed to be leaving behind us? Charlie, understandably, is less than happy about all this. One great line in the play is where he shouts, 'They found a new way to keep Jews out: They just made us white instead!'

As I write (May 2019), Oxford University has just announced that for the first time in its 900 year history, it will offer places to some students from backgrounds that are considered to be disadvantaged, accepting lower grades from them than are required from other students. This, as you might expect, is part of Oxford's plan to boost diversity in its student body. This policy brings Oxford into line with some other top British universities which have similar schemes in place.

The White curriculum

It's not only that the people in the best universities are too white; the curriculum is also said to be too White! Would Western civilisation be a good idea, as Gandhi is reputed to have said, or is the proper attitude to Western Civilisation—boo, hiss! That's pretty much the attitude of many Western leftists and pretty much the level of the intellectual content of their rejection of it. The idea that the study of Western civilisation is something worthy of support seems to be anathema even to some of those who occupy positions in that most Western of civilised institutions, the university. The irony of this frisson seems to escape them. One of these sceptics is Professor Coleborne, Head of Humanities and Social Sciences at the University of Newcastle. According to her, Western civilisation doesn't reflect the diversity (think skin colour diversity) of the classroom of the modern university. That implies, it seems she thinks, that non-white students shouldn't be required to study what are essentially White values. Why is this? Because Western civilisation is associated in the minds of leftists exclusively with supremacy, exploitation, oppression and privilege and with Whiteness, especially with Whiteness. That the Head of Humanities and Social Sciences at a university would link Western Civilisation primarily to race is illustrative of the extent to which identity politics has spread its tentacles from the wider society into the hallowed halls of the university.

Mr Jason Osamede Okundaye, writing in connection with the so-called 'decolonisation of education' fuss in Cambridge, said, 'Diversity of thought is vital if universities wish to retain intellectual integrity.' (Okundaye 2017) Indeed! I couldn't agree more. But this ringing and entirely praiseworthy pronouncement is slightly at odds with the purpose of the decolonisation agenda. The activists don't appear to want diversity of thought, they want writers on the curriculum who have *their* skin colour or ethnicity! It's hard to see how race or sex would matter if decolonisation was about diversity of thought! Mr Okundaye's idea of what diversity of thought consists in links thought-patterns to different races, not to different individuals, leading to the ridiculous result that all male European writers, however different they may be from one another, form one homogeneous block!

At Reed College, to take a specific example, it's not just courses on Western civilisation that are the problem but the entire curriculum! That said, one particular course, Hum 110, is alleged to participate 'in the narrative of white supremacy.' It is Eurocentric and should be changed to reflect what one student (I'll call her Janice) calls 'the lived experience of people of colour.' It is also too White and does not sufficiently represent non-white people in history, art history and English. Some of the academic staff appear to agree with Janice. One chemistry professor will discuss research only by people of colour, women or those with maximum intersectional privilege.

Of particular interest is the conversation Janice had with one professor, if it can properly be described as a conversation and not as it appears, as a presentation of an ultimatum. When Janice made her point that the humanities programme as a whole perpetuated racism, the professor disagreed, only to be told that it didn't matter what she said! The judgement as to whether the programme perpetuated racism could be made only by students of colour and they had decided it was racist. Epistemic privilege with a vengeance.

And there you have it. Experience, however peculiar, fabricated or irrational is the ultimate judge of fact. When Janice was challenged that she was not willing to allow others to have opinions she became emotional and expressed the view that opinions such as these were what led to injustice. 'When I tell people that I feel pain and it's coming from what they say, people don't want to be accountable for that pain. They say, "I'm not the villain". But, according to her, they *are* the villains in the piece by refusing to acknowledge their racism! Disagreement with Janice is not, it seems, a morally defensible option. Failure to engage with her and her companions in protest is tantamount to 'participating in the pain against these bodies of colour.' According to Janice, 'The biggest thing I've faced as a black woman is silencing.' Given the licence she has been given to protest, disrupt and harass, this claim seems antecedently unlikely to be true.

Happily, it is now beginning to appear that some of the other students at Reed who, unaccountably seem to believe that they are at university to get an education, are losing patience with Janice and her protesting cohort. At the first Hum 110 lecture, Janice and two supporters introduced themselves to the class and were challenged. One young woman said, 'We would like the opportunity to attend class before we're told what's in it'. The crowd burst into seven seconds of raucous applause. A video captures the stunned faces of the demonstrators as they left the auditorium.

It's generally accepted that it's not a good idea to judge a book by its cover but in the eyes of some diversiphiles, it might just be a good idea to judge a book by the skin colour of its author. A former professor at one of the London universities has made a political decision not to cite any non-white authors. 'Surely not!' I hear you exclaim! Well, you're right. What actually happened was that the professor in question actually made a political decision not to cite any *white* authors. Oh well, that's all right then! The professor, Sara Ahmed, a one-time professor of race and cultural studies (yes, yes, I know, it's not an academic discipline but that's what passes for a subject in universities today) took this decision because she believes that white men cite white men and she sees 'whiteness spilled all over the pages', something that she says is invisible to those who inhabit Whiteness. Of course, Ms Ahmed is free to cite and not cite whoever she wants in her writings but her policy is, not to put too fine a point on it, racist. It is also deeply self-contradictory given that one of the aims of the identitarians such as she is to destabilise binary distinctions, one of which, of course, is white/black. Do I have to point out the obvious, that her decision is predicated precisely on the black/white binary? And I would ask you to suppress the thought that Ahmed's action constitutes an astonishing act of intellectual conceit, prejudging and dismissing the work of others from the oxygen-free moral high ground. Of course, there are distinct advantages to her decision in that she can now save a lot of time that would otherwise have had to be devoted to reading the work of others. Put to one side the whole bizarre policy of the use of citations by promotions committees as a measure of academic worth. The point has been made repeatedly that an academic's work might be cited plentifully because it is egregiously bad, but that's a problem for another day. But Ahmed's policy focuses not on what is said but on the colour of the skin of the person saying it. Except in the most trivial of senses, there is, of course, no white philosophy or black philosophy, any more than there is an Irish philosophy or an English philosophy or a Lancashire philosophy or a Timbuktu philosophy and the same applies to any other reputable academic discipline. It should be obvious that any professor who refuses to cite the work of another scholar purely on racial grounds is deeply racist.

Afterword and Summary

Magna est veritas et prevalebit

Even the weariest river winds somewhere safe to sea and so too our discussion of free speech and tolerance has likewise wound its way to an end. One reader of this book in its manuscript stage said that when she had finished it she felt depressed! Not that she thought the book was bad, she hastened to add, rather that the situation it described was worse than she had ever imagined. The position of free speech and tolerance in our contemporary world is bad and it is likely to get worse in the immediate future so that depression is a perfectly understandable emotional reaction. But the aim of the book is not to depress its readers but to alert them to the existential threats to free speech and tolerance and to encourage all those among them who value being able to speak freely and who want to tolerate others and be tolerated in turn to fight against the waves of repression.

Even though this book is not long, I have touched on so many topics that even the most attentive reader might be forgiven for not recalling the overall thrust of the argument. Here, then, is a brief reminder in summary form of some of the scenic highlights of our intellectual journey.

• The maxim 'My House, My Rules' (MHMR) is derived from the Zero Aggression Principle (ZAP) and gives us a principled basis upon which to regulate free speech, making the regulation of speech a matter for the owners of property. On or with my property I can, with certain minimal exceptions, say what I please; you, on the other hand, may exclusively determine what can be said and done on your property. Having a right to speak freely doesn't carry with it the right to make use of another person's property or resources to enable you to express your views.

• Free speech can be legally regulated where it shades over into action and such action is clearly criminal when evaluated by the standard of the ZAP. There is no justification for civil laws inhibiting free speech. The social ills for which the law on defamation purports to be a guard and a remedy can be alleviated in ways consistent with the ZAP.

• Hate is an emotion and should not, in itself, be a matter for law. Hate crime is thought crime since punishing a certain criminal action that is accompanied or motivated by hate more severely than that same crime committed without hate makes the hate the object of the greater severity in punishment. The relevant mental element in crime is intention, not motive.

• Laws that mandate certain specific forms of speech under legal penalty are a clear violation of the ZAP.

• Blasphemy is not a matter for the law. All systems of thought—religions included—may be criticised, reasonably or unreasonably, politely or crudely.

• University authorities have the right to prohibit people from speaking on their campuses if they so choose, just as any property owner has the right to control the disposition of his property. Whether they are right to do so is another matter, especially given that the pursuit of truth is a constituent element of what a university is.

• On the libertarian principle of free association/dissociation, any group of people, students or otherwise, can make their own arrangements for membership and include or exclude whoever they wish and allow or disallow topics for discussion as they see fit, but the idea that the university as a whole should be a 'safe space', a place of emotional and intellectual placidity into which no disturbing ideas are permitted to intrude, is totally at odds with the very nature of the university.

• We must distinguish between intellectual (in)tolerance and practical (in)tolerance. Practical intolerance is not a necessary consequence of intellectual intolerance, nor does practical tolerance necessitate intellectual tolerance. If others have beliefs that we think are false or engage in actions that we find mildly distasteful or reprehensible or even repulsive, we are not entitled to use force to prevent them believing or acting as they do unless their beliefs or actions constitute aggression.

• Tolerance contains an ineluctably negative element inasmuch as we do not tolerate what we like, respect or admire. Tolerance is tolerance and not validation, respect, acceptance, admiration or appreciation.

• The currently fashionable dogmas of diversity, inclusion and equality are forms of practical intolerance. These dogmas rest upon the empirically ungrounded assumption that, absent human malignity, the proportion of Xs, Ys and Zs in private or government employment or any trade, activity, profession would mirror the proportion of Xs, Ys and Zs in the general population.

• For diversity dogmatists in the university there must be diversity everywhere and in everything—except in thought. The contemporary university, far from being a bastion of free speech and tolerance is a significant vehicle for the promotion of the new intolerance.

Verba ultima

Free speech is an aspect of the freedom that belongs to us as rational beings to act as we see fit within the scope of the ZAP and its associated maxims. It is therefore a right, not a reward for good behaviour or a privilege for conformity to what someone else considers to be indispensable social and political norms. Who should get to speak freely? Everyone! Free speech is not just for you and for your friends but for your foes and for your faultfinders. Within the parameters of the ZAP, tolerance is a minimally necessary condition of peaceful co-existence in a flawed and fallen world.

References

Adams, Alexander. (2018) 'Hate-speech laws help only the powerful.' *Spiked*. Available online.

Ahmed, Qanta. (2018) 'The ECHR's ruling on defaming Mohammed is bad news for Muslims.' *The Spectator*. Available online.

Akehurst, Christopher. (2018) 'Three little words that mean "shut up!"' *The Spectator*. Available online.

Anon. (1996) 'A sign of the times.' *The New Criterion*. Available online.

Anon. (2015) 'On some uses of "but".' *The New Criterion*. Available online.

Anon. (2016) 'Safe from "Safe Spaces": On the rare good sense of a college administrator.' *The New Criterion*, vol. 34, no. 9. Available online.

Anon. (2017) 'Evergreen: Top 20 Monstrous Moments.' Available at <https://www.youtube.com/watch?v=8YnSYvhSeyI>.

Anon. (2017a) 'Academic follies (still cont'd).' *The New Criterion*. Available online.

Anon. (2017b) 'Why the Left hates tolerance.' *The New Criterion*. Available online.

Anon. (2017c) 'The Google Memo: Four Scientists Respond.' *Quillette*. Available online

Anon. (2018) 'Whip out 18C.' *The Spectator* (Australia). Available online.

Anon. (2018a) 'Oxford professor "told to retire at 67 to allow diversity".' *The Daily Telegraph*. Available online.

Ash, Timothy Garton. (2016) *Free Speech*. London: Atlantic Books.

BBC News. (2017) 'Oxford vice-chancellor criticised over homosexuality comments.' Available online.

BBC News. (2018) 'Hollywood films "had fewer LGBT characters in 2017".' Available online.

Cascone, Sarah. (2018) 'Is Damien Hirst's Latest Series a Ripoff of an Aboriginal Australian Artist. See the Works Side-by-Side.' New York: Editions. Available online.

Casey, Gerard. (2017) *Freedom's Progress? A History of Political Thought*. Exeter: Imprint Academic.

Choudary, Anjem. (2015) 'People know the consequences: Opposing view.' *USA Today*. Available online.

Chua, Amy. (2018) 'How America's identity politics went from inclusion to division.' *The Guardian*. Available online.

Clark, Robert C. (1995) 'Harvard Law School Memorandum: Sexual Harassment Guidelines.' Available at The 'Lectric Law Library at <https://www.lectlaw.com/files/edu01.htm>.

Cobley, Ben. (2018) *The Tribe: The Liberal-Left and the System of Diversity*. Exeter: Societas (Imprint Academic).

Cohen, Nick. (2012) *You Can't Read This Book: Censorship in an Age of Freedom*. London: Fourth Estate.

Cohen, Tanya. (2015) '#NotMyAmerica: It's Time For Americans To Stop Confusing Freedom Of Speech With Hate Speech.' *Thought Catalog*. Available online.

College Factual. (no date) 'Arizona Demographics: How diverse is it?' Available at <https://www.collegefactual.com/colleges/university-of-arizona/student-life/diversity>.

Cook, Cody, Rebecca Diamond, Jonathan Hall et al. (2019) 'The Gender earnings Gap in the Gig Economy: Evidence from over a Million Rideshare Drivers.' *Working Paper No. 3637*, Stanford Graduate School of Business, 2018. Available online.

Damore, James. (2017) 'Google's Ideological Echo Chamber: How Bias Clouds our Thinking about Diversity and Inclusion.' Available online.

Davies, Jon Gower. (2010) *A New Inquisition: Religious Persecution in Britain Today*. London: Civitas.

Dineen, Tana. (1999) *Manufacturing Victims*. London: Little, Brown Book Group.

Dinsmore, Emily. (2018) 'Young people have never had it so good.'

Spiked. Available online.

Doward, Jamie. (2019) 'Psychologist to be investigated over opposition to LGBT lessons.' *The Guardian*. Available online.

Driscoll, Margarette. (2019) '"There is a climate of intimidation at British universities – we are afraid to speak about anything controversial."' *The Daily Telegraph*.

Dunant, Sarah. (ed.) (1994) *The War of the Words: The Political Correctness Debate*. London: Virago Press.

Dworkin, Ronald. (1997) *Freedom's Law*. Cambridge, Massachusetts: Harvard University Press.

Eberstadt, Mary. (2015) 'The New Intolerance.' *First Things*. Available online.

Eberstadt, Mary. (2016) *It's Dangerous to Believe: Religious Freedom and Its Enemies*. New York: Harper.

Emba, Christine. (2018) 'One deleted column does not a war on free speech make.' *The Washington Post*. Available online.

European Commission. (2019) 'Countering illegal hate speech online – EU Code of Conduct ensures swift response.' Available online.

European Court of Human Rights. (25 October 2018) 'Judgement E.S. v. Austria – conviction for a critic of Islam did not violate Article 10.' Available online.

Family Policy Institute of Washington. (2016) 'Gender Identity: Can a 5'9, White Guy Be a 6'5, Chinese Woman?' Available at <https://www.youtube.com/watch?v=xfO1veFs6Ho>.

Farrington, Allen. (2019) 'After Academia.' *Quillette*. Available online.

Featherstone, Liza. (2018) 'I Think My Friend is a Jordan Peterson Fan. What Should I Do?' *The Nation*. Available online.

Fish, Stanley. (1994) *There's No Such Thing as Free Speech: And It's a Good Thing Too*. New York: Oxford University Press.

Fox, Claire. (2016) *'I Find That Offensive!'* London: Biteback Books.

Fukuyama, Francis. (2018) *Identity: Contemporary Identity Politics and the Struggle for Recognition*. London: Profile Books.

Furedi, Frank. (2011) 'Can we tolerate intolerance?' *Independent*. Available online.

Furedi, Frank. (2011a) *On Tolerance: A Defence of Moral Independence.*' London: Continuum.

Furedi, Frank. (2011b) 'Don't blame tolerance for this multicultural mess.' *Spiked*. Available online.

Furedi, Frank. (2012) 'On tolerance.' *Policy*, Vol. 28 No. 2. Available online.

Furedi, Frank. (2017) *What's Happened to the University?: A Sociological Exploration of its Infantilisation.* London: Routledge.

Furedi, Frank. (2018) 'A culture of bullying? Grow up.' *Spiked.* Available online.

Gilley, Bruce. (2017) 'The case for colonialism' *Third World Quarterly*. Available online.

Goodenough, Tom. (2019) 'What happened when an innocent Christian preacher was accused of Islamophobia?' *The Spectator.* Available online.

Gross, Paul R. and Norman Levitt. (1994) *Higher Superstition: The Academic Left and its Quarrels with Science.* Baltimore, Maryland: Johns Hopkins University Press.

Guinness, Os. (2000) *Time for Truth: Living Free in a World of Lies, Hype, & Spin.* Grand Rapids, Michigan: Baker Books.

Hannan, Daniel. (2019) 'Do you have to be Left-wing to study at the University of Cambridge?' *The Daily Telegraph.*

Hart, Adrian. (2014) *That's Racist!: How the Regulation of Speech and Thought Divides Us All.* Exeter: Imprint Academic.

Himmelfarb, Gertrude. (1995) 'The Gender Card Loses.' *The Weekly Standard.* Available online.

Hinsliff, Gaby. (2017) 'If millennials are wary of free speech, who can blame them?' *The Guardian.* Available online.

Hinsliff, Gaby. (2018) 'Could hating men become a crime?' *The Guardian.* Available online.

Hull, Crispin. (2019) 'Israel Folau and the importance of protecting free speech' *The Canberra Times.* Available online.

Hume, Mick. (2015) *Trigger Warning: Is the Fear of Being Offensive Killing Free Speech?* London: William Collins.

Hymas, Charles (2018) 'Ageism could be classed as a hate crime, Sajid Javid poised to announce.' *The Daily Telegraph.*

Jacobs, James B. and Kimberly Potter. (1998) *Hate Crimes: Criminal Law & Identity Politics*. New York: Oxford University Press.

Javid, Sajid. (2018) 'I've been called a coconut and worse so I know how important it is to stamp out hate crime.' *The Daily Telegraph*. Available online.

Jones, Edgar. (2017) 'A traumatic history.' *Spiked*. Available online.

Jussim, Lee. (2017) 'The Google Memo: Race and Gender Gaps and their solutions.' *Psychology Today*. Available online.

Kennedy, Randy. (21 March 2017) 'White Artist's Painting of Emmett Till at Whitney Biennial Draws Protests.' New York; *New York Times*. Available online.

King, Richard. (2013) *On Offence: The Politics of Indignation*. London: Scribe.

Kors, Alan Charles. (2008) 'On the Sadness of Higher Education.' *The Wall Street Journal*. Available online.

Lal, Deepak. (2012) *Lost Causes: The Retreat from Classical Liberalism*. London: Biteback.

Leith, Sam. (2018) 'Conservatives are wrong about free speech.' *The Spectator*. Available onlin.

Liptak, Adam. (2018) 'How Conservatives Weaponized the First Amendment.' *The New York Times*. Available online.

Luce, Edward. (2018) *The Retreat of Western Liberalism*. London: Abacus.

Lukianoff, Greg. (2014) *Unlearning Liberty: Campus Censorship and the End of American Debate*. London: Encounter Books.

Lynch, Frederick R. (1997) *The Diversity Machine: The Drive to Change the 'White Male Workplace'*. New York: The Free Press.

MacDonald, Heather. (2018) *The Diversity Delusion: How Race and Gender Pandering Corrupt the University and Undermine Our Culture*. New York: St Martin's Press.

Mansfield, Harvey C. *Manliness*. New Haven, Connecticut: Yale University Press.

Mayberry, Katherine. (1994) 'White Feminists Who Study Black Writers.' *Chronicle of Higher Education*.

Mill, John Stuart. (1991) 'On Liberty,' in *On Liberty and Other Essays*, (ed. John Gray). Oxford: Oxford University Press. [Oxford

World's Classics]

Murray, Douglas. (2019) 'Cambridge has become the epicentre of the "wokeness" epidemic plaguing our universities.' *The Daily Telegraph*.

Nagle, Angela. (2017) *Kill All Normies*. Winchester: Zero Books.

National Archives. *Defamation Act 2013*. Available online.

Nayna, Mike. (2019) 'Brett Weinstein, Heather Heying & the Evergreen Equity Council.' YouTube video, available at <https://www.youtube.com/watch?v=FH2WeWgcSMk>.

Nayna, Mike. (2019) 'Teaching to Transgress.' YouTube video, available at <https://www.youtube.com/watch?v=A0W9Qb-kX8Cs>.

Newman, Maurice. (2019) 'Free speech: a right-wing conspiracy?' *The Spectator*. Available online.

Okundaye, Jason Osamede. (2017) 'The "decolonise" Cambridge row is yet another attack on students of colour.' *The Guardian*. Available online.

Olusoga, David. (2018) 'We risk losing slices of our past if we don't root our racism in our universities.' *The Guardian*. Available online.

O'Neill, Brendan. (2015) 'The "Yale snowflakes": who made these monsters?' *Spiked*. Available online.

O'Neill, Brendan. (2017) 'After London: let's start talking about Islam.' *Spiked*. Available online.

O'Neill, Brendan (2018) 'Why we must have the right to call Allah gay.' *Spiked*. Available online.

Prince's Trust. (2018) 'Youth Index 2018.' Available online.

Pryce-Jones, David. (2014) 'On the frontlines of free speech.' *The New Criterion*. Available online.

Puzo, Mario. (1998/1969) *The Godfather*. London: Arrow.

Robinson, Nathan J. (2017) 'A Quick Reminder of Why Colonialism was Bad.' *Current Affairs*. Available online.

Rose, Eleanor. (2017) 'King's College London deploys "Safe Space Marshals" to ensure students "don't have their feelings hurt" at talks.' Available online.

Saunders, Alison. (2017) 'Hate is hate. Online abusers must be dealt with harshly.' *The Guardian.* Available online.

Shortt, Rupert. (2013) *Christianophobia: A Faith under Attack.* London: Random House Group.

Slater, Tom. (ed.) (2016) *Unsafe Space: The Crisis of Free Speech on Campus.* London: Palgrave Macmillan.

Sleeper, Jim. (1998) *Liberal Racism: How Fixating on Race Subverts the American Dream.* London: Penguin.

Smith, Steven D. (2018) *Pagans & Christians in the City: Culture Wars from the Tiber to the Potomac.* Grand Rapids, Michigan: Eerdmans.

Sowell, Thomas. (2018) *Discrimination and Disparities.* New York: Basic Books.

Steyn, Mark. (2010) 'Live Free or Die.' *The New Criterion.* Available online.

Stoet, Gijsbert and David C. Geary. (2018) 'The Gender-Equality Paradox in Science, Technology, Engineering, and Mathematics Education.' *Psychological Science,* 29, pp. 581-93. Available online.

Strossen, Nadine. (2018) *Hate: Why We Should Resist it with Free Speech, Not Censorship.* New York: Oxford University Press.

Supreme Court. (10 October 2018) 'Press Summary.' Available online.

Tettenborn, Andrew. (2017) 'Now universities police speech off campus.' *Spiked.* Available online.

Toope, Stephen J. (2019) 'Rescindment of visiting fellowship statement from Vice-Chancellor Professor Stephen J. Toope.' Available online.

Turner, Camilla. (2019) 'Oxford ends women-only fellowship as University rules that it breaches equality law.' *The Daily Telegraph.* Available online.

Twitter. (23 February 2019) 'Eye on Anti-Semitism.' Available online.

Vonnegut, Kurt. (1972) *Welcome to the Monkey House.* St Albans, Herts: Panther.

Wasserman, Elizabeth. (2015) 'Rise of the femsplainers.' *National Post.* Available online.

Whelan, Ella. (2017) 'On the therapeutic state.' *Spiked*. Available online.

Whelan, Ella. (2018) 'No, women are not damaged goods.' *Spiked*. Available online.

Williams, Joanna. (2016) *Academic Freedom in an Age of Conformity*. London: Palgrave Macmillan.

Wood, Peter W. (2003) *Diversity: The Invention of a Concept*. San Francisco: Encounter Books.

Wood, Peter W. (2017) 'Seven types of suppression.' *The New Criterion*. Available online.

Young, Toby (2019) 'Jordan Peterson and mob rule at the University of Cambridge.' *Spectator USA*. Available online.

YouTube. (8 February 2013) 'The Devil, is he all bad?' Available at <https://www.youtube.com/watch?v=EWa3LyvFOdc>.

www.ingramcontent.com/pod-product-compliance
Lightning Source LLC
Chambersburg PA
CBHW071052280326
41928CB00050B/2259